LEADERSHIP
AND
LIBERTY

PIECES OF THE PUZZLE

CHRIS BRADY AND ORRIN WOODWARD

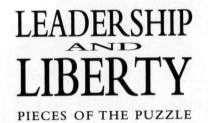

LEADERSHIP AND LIBERTY

PIECES OF THE PUZZLE

By Chris Brady and Orrin Woodward

Second Edition, September 2011

Published by:

Obstaclés Press
4072 Market Place Drive
Flint, MI 48507

lifeleadership.com

ISBN: 978-0-9858020-1-1

Cover design and layout by Norm Williams

Printed in the United States of America

DEDICATION

This book is dedicated to all those who
cherish freedom and adhere to the concept of
liberty and justice for all.

ACKNOWLEDGEMENTS

Any attempt to illuminate the deep sister topics of leadership and liberty would be impossible without, as Sir Isaac Newton quipped, "standing on the shoulders of giants." We are certainly indebted to experts, leaders, and authors both contemporary and historical for their insights, experiences, wisdom, and examples. For a recommended reading list of just a handful of our favorite works by these giants, please see the back of the book. For ease of reference each has been classified according to the categories represented in this book.

As for the many contributors critical to the success of a project such as this, we would like to begin by thanking our wives, Terri Brady and Laurie Woodward, who continue to inspire us with their daily examples of thoughtful service and leadership. We would truly like to read a book by them someday!

The entire staff at Obstaclés Press also deserves recognition. Their dedication and professionalism is incredible. This begins with our good friend and COO Rob Hallstrand. We know how much you all do behind the scenes, and we appreciate it. Know that your dedication is making a difference in a lot of lives. Norm Williams also gets our thanks for the tireless application of his artistic talents in making us look good! Thank you also to the other founders of LIFE Leadership: Tim and Amy Marks, George and Jill Guzzardo, Bill and Jackie Lewis, Claude and Lana Hamilton, and Dan and Lisa Hawkins. You are the best team of leaders we've ever seen. We

We would also like to thank our parents, Jim and Gayle Brady, and Bud (deceased) and Kathy Woodward for your constant encouragement and belief.

Most importantly, we wish to give all the glory to our Lord and Savior Jesus Christ. Everything we have and will ever accomplish is by His grace.

CONTENTS

Introduction 11

ATTITUDE AND SUCCESS
Attitude: They Could Have Been Great 13
Live While You're Alive 33
Putting Gas in Your Tank 52
Moments of Greatness 69
"On Call" and the Technology Addiction 85
Daily Disciplines to Success 103
The Power of Audio Learning 123
Reading 133
Practice Your Craft 141
Overcoming Criticism 150
The Power of Goal Setting 177
Hard Work 155
Find Your Authentic Swing 165
Give Them Something to Shout About 175
If We Had Less Would We Do More? 181
Romance and Persistent Cheeriness 189
Sharpen the Saw 191
The Character to Be a Character 197
The Excellent Man 199
There is No Ready 201
We Created Them 206
Key Questions 208
Finishing Well 228

PEOPLE SKILLS AND PRINCIPLES
People Skills - Victory Over Self 15
Get History With People 35
Give Validation 71
Become a Cultivator 72
Blind Spots 87

TABLE OF CONTENTS

Communication 110
Friendship, The Art of the Heart 127
Help Others Win 135
Relationships 90
Why People Stay in Community 167
The Power of a Team 193
The Temptation of Removing Human Freedom 218

LEADERSHIP PRINCIPLES
Hunger, the Fuel of Your Leadership Engine 16
The Education of a Leader 55
Encouraging in a Discouraging World 51
Leaders Build Relationships 90
Anyone Could Lead Perfect People 112
Dream Big. Serve Hard. Live Large 129
Courage of Your Convictions or Cowardice of
Your Comforts 137
Drearies vs. Leaders 146
What is the Upside of Adversity? 157
The Leadership Tractor Pull 159
It's All In Your Thinking 169
Heart of Fire and Spirit of Honor 177
Leadership Conduct, the World is Watching 183
The Uniform of Leadership is Thick Skin 195
Leadership Hunger 202
Mentoring - Learning to Think Through Life 209
Leadership Feedback 211
Leave a Legacy 222

HISTORICAL LEADERSHIP ILLUSTRATIONS
They Were There 18
Burgoyne's Proclamation 37
Actions Accumulate - Caesar Augustus 57
James "Buster" Douglas vs. Mike Tyson -
A Real Life David vs. Goliath 74
Churchill Overcomes 92

TABLE OF CONTENTS

The Lesson of Initiative: Thomas Cochrane and
the Capture of the Gamo 114
Launching an Armada: Buyer Beware 214

THE HISTORY OF LIBERTY
A Republic, If You Can Keep It 20
Foundations of Freedom Part I 39
Foundations of Freedom Part II 60
Our American Heritage - Educating the
Electorate is the Key 76
Do Leaders Make History or Does History
Make Leaders? 97
Eternal Vigilance 118
Some Fights are Worth Making 138
Not All Revolutions are Equal 148
Symbols of the Oppression of Liberty 162
A Fundamental Change in Thinking 172
Cynicism and the False Belief in Progress 179
Junkets on the Ship of State 185
Softness and Socialism 204
Freedom Under Fire - From Republic to Empire to ? 230

ECONOMICS
Booms, Bust and Balderdash -
Inflationary Business Cycles 24
The Curse of Wealth Unearned 42
Austrian Economics, Peter Schiff and the Bailouts 63
Unsound Money System Needed by
Government for Wealth Confiscation 79
Government Spending, Keynesian Economics
and Political Responsibility 100
Confiscation or Incentive 120

POLITICS AND GOVERNANCE
How Much Can We Carry? 28
Tyranny Falls 45
A Thesis 65

TABLE OF CONTENTS

Ignorance Destroys Beauty 66
Democracy in the NBA 81
Partial Birth Abortions - The Crime
Against Conscience? 107
Big Government Goose Killer 125
False Presuppositions 131
More Government = Wrong Answer 212
Cycle of Democracy and Alexander Fraser Tyler 234

Suggested Reading List 243

INTRODUCTION

As we've written before, leaders attack the status quo. They cannot remain silent in the face of disorder, disunity, disgrace or injustice. In today's economic, social, and political climate, in which precious treasures of freedom and liberty won for us by the sacrifice and excruciating effort of our ancestors are increasingly being eroded and dismantled, we find ourselves unable to remain silent. What follows in these pages is the response to the unacceptable status quo with which we find ourselves confronted every day.

In the course of building a business across the North American continent we are continually exposed to the results that stem from the loss of respect for the individual, an erosion of the rule of law, a growing power of the international media to shape thought rather than inform it, a slide toward socialism and the welfare state, apathy among the voting public, special interest group domination, big business special deals, and the overall loss of freedom for the unsuspecting citizen. These may sound like mere concepts and categories, or objects for theoretical discussion, and perhaps even topics unsuitable for polite conversation. We can assure the reader, however, that they are real issues with concrete ramifications for everyone. Nobody lives outside the effects of poor government, irresponsible economics, bad policy, socialism, and bureaucracy gone wild, not even those who believe themselves to be the recipient or benefactor of government largesse. Everyone is affected, and no one more so than the unsuspecting person who is daily consumed with earning his or her living, fulfilling his or her responsibilities, and doing his or her best just to make it through a complicated and unfair world.

This brings us to the topic of leadership. Everyone will be called upon to lead at some point, and in fact, at many points in life.

INTRODUCTION

These calls will be for both big things and small. Some will endure for the long haul and others will be only for a season. Additionally, everyone has the ability to lead in some capacity and in some endeavor. Although we are each endowed with a diversity of gifts and experiences, backgrounds and heritages, we all have the ability to grow in our leadership ability and effectiveness. This was the theme of our book *Launching a Leadership Revolution*. That book was intended to inspire and train leaders from all walks of life, to unleash the power within them to affect positive change through the timeless principles of leadership, and to accomplish all this through the understanding and exercising of the Five Levels of Influence. In our follow up book, *Leadership Tidbits and Treasures*, we compiled our most popular articles, which had first appeared on our blogs (*orrinwoodwardblog.com* and *chrisbrady.com*), of application and background, upon which the *Launching a Leadership Revolution* book was based.

Next in the series of works on leadership, this book is designed to build upon *Launching a Leadership Revolution* and *Leadership Tidbits and Treasures* by not only reviewing timeless leadership principles, but by focusing them upon leadership as applied to the concepts of liberty and freedom, and specifically, to winning back much of what has been lost in our lands. As we hope to make implicitly clear in the pages to follow, an educated and informed electorate is the key to preserving freedom. Our intent is that this book will not only inform and educate, but equip leaders both new and experienced alike, to make an increasing difference in the fight for the first principles of freedom. As Thomas Jefferson wrote, "If a nation expects to be ignorant and free . . . it expects what never was and never will be."

Our world needs leadership as never before. We pray this book will inspire and assist you in playing your part.

Chris Brady and Orrin Woodward
Killarney, Ireland
April 2009

12

ATTITUDE:
THEY COULD HAVE BEEN GREAT!

Almost anything that can be said about the topic of attitude sounds like a cliché, as though it's all been said before. Still, I wonder, why is having a good attitude so rare in our society? We have the highest standard of living in the world, the highest of anybody in history, better health, better technology, better comforts, longer life-expectancy, etc., but none of this seems to produce a spirit of gratitude.

Having a good attitude has to start with an understanding that we are blessed. We must take stock of the great things God has bestowed upon us if we are to have a proper outlook on the one life we have to live.

Further, a proper attitude shows respect for others. The "Accept, Approve, Appreciate" principles from Les Giblin's *How to Have Power and Confidence in Dealing with People* still apply. People have a basic need to be accepted by others. Then they seek approval. Finally, they want to be appreciated. Is this really so hard to give?

Of course, attitude is also comprised of one's outlook about the future. Let's face it, pessimism is repulsive, plain and simple. Nobody likes to be around a person who is negative, who brings others down, and who points out what's wrong with the world. Worse to be around are the types that criticize, condemn, and complain about other people.

Wisdom comes from examined experience, reading the scriptures, prayer, and study.

Know-it-alls are really just people with bad attitudes about the competency of others. Do such people really think they have a lock on knowledge, or that they are that much smarter than others?

When it comes down to it, people with bad attitudes just don't have a proper perspective on things. What this really demonstrates is a lack of wisdom. Wisdom comes from examined experience, reading the scriptures, prayer, and study. Unfortunately, most people partake in none of these. They assign blame to others for their failures instead of learning the lessons those failures have to teach. They don't pray, they don't read good books (no time, of course), and they certainly don't read the Bible. Being uninformed, they see fit to take only their *own* counsel on matters in life, and amplify their incorrect conclusions through their bad attitude. At this point, the rest of us are allowed to share in it!

In the movie *The Kid*, starring Bruce Willis, the girlfriend of the main character finally gets fed up with his bad attitude. Turning around before walking away, she says, "Do you know what the saddest thing is? You could have been great!" That's how it is with bad attitudes. It's not so much that they bring other people down; although they do. It's not so much that they are a waste of time;

although they are. It's that they deprive the person of greatness. They fill the void where greatness should reside. Rest assured that pessimism, negative thoughts, ingratitude, and critical spirits will never lead to greatness. And the saddest thing is that for everyone who has succumbed to the temptation of selling out to negative, "They could have been great!"

Attitude is reframing the thinking about the events in your life to empower you towards victory, instead of disempowering you towards defeat. – Orrin Woodward

PEOPLE SKILLS: VICTORY OVER *SELF*

The longer I am in leadership the more certain I am that people skills are the necessary oil to make everything run smooththly. Why are there so many people conflicts as organizations get bigger? I have a real simple answer: Self.

When people focus on only their win and not the win for all parties involved, there will be conflict. Individuals under stress will tend to revert to protection of self and lose their emotional intelligence. A great leader must rise above stress, setbacks, and self-concern to focus on serving others anyway. Leaders focus on the entire picture and not just what is best for them. As you hear about people skills and develop them more and more in yourself, you may be tempted to think, "This will be easy." I promise, when you attempt to implement people skills into your daily habits you will find that "self" is the biggest enemy. Alexander the Great and Julius Caesar conquered much of the known world, but never conquered *self*. If you desire to be truly great, the biggest victory you will ever have is the victory over self.

I encourage everyone to focus their energies on improving self because this is one area directly under your control. You will realize how futile it is to change others when you understand how tough a battle you have just to change yourself. Now that we have identified the real battle, go forward with confidence and obtain the victory that leads to all the others.

15

HUNGER, THE FUEL OF YOUR LEADERSHIP ENGINE

There are a lot of terms that could be used to describe a leader, but hunger is a primary prerequisite. Why is hunger so central to becoming a leader? Because leadership is all about change.

The word *lead* is a verb describing the influence of others to a place the leader has often not even visited himself. This requires the ability to deal with change effectively; personally and externally as well as organizationally. Helping others change and grow is a large part of what leaders spend their time doing. Through this collective change comes advancement and achievement. None of this can happen unless the leader has a larger supply of hunger to change than the fear or complacency that threatens to stop him.

"When the pain of staying the same becomes greater than the pain of changing, you'll change!"

As the saying goes, "When the pain of staying the same becomes greater than the pain of changing, you'll change!" Hunger describes the positive side of the coin that has "pain" on the other side. In other words, when your hunger outgrows the power that the status quo has over you, you will change and grow as a leader.

Whenever we miss goals, stop advancing, and fall upon stalled periods in our life, it is usually because we have allowed our hunger to flag. We have allowed the tanks that fuel our leadership engine to run dry. Try to envision hunger as a liquid fuel you store in your mind. To keep your engine running continuously, you will need to supply and re-supply it with proper fuel. This is actually a discipline. As a leader you must build your hunger muscles and keep them strong. How is this done? By reviewing your primary motivations on a regular basis, associating with like-minded motivated people, reading good books, studying the scriptures so you keep an eternal perspective on your life's work, having concrete goals, and keeping in constant touch with your purpose and cause. It also comes from finding someone else to serve and love, and being active in the pursuit of your purpose so you build skills and gain confidence and momentum. Leaders that fall behind in their results are usually lax in exercising these key hunger disciplines.

Having proper questions to ask yourself also helps. Here are a few:

1. Who am I going to serve today?
2. What steps am I going to take toward my dream today?
3. What is my purpose in life?
4. What special skills has God given me that point me to my purpose?
5. What activities make me "come alive?"
6. What dreams or achievements can I think about and focus upon to get myself excited about achievement?
7. What kind of legacy am I leaving with the way I am living my life each day?
8. What is the highest picture I can generate in my mind's eye of the kind of person God is fashioning me into for His glory?
9. Am I making the most of my gifts and time?
10. Ten years from today, what would I wish I had been doing?

Don't expect your leadership engine to run properly if you starve it of fuel. Give it the good, high octane stuff all the time. And if you don't, you shouldn't be surprised if it starts sputtering.

THEY WERE THERE

"Why do you like history?" someone once asked, "It's so dull; dates and places and names I can't remember."

Somewhere along the line in this person's life he or she was given the wrong sample of the subject of history. This led to a grave misunderstanding. It would be like giving you an ice-cream sandwich you spit out because you don't like the taste of the paper. If no one ever unwrapped it properly for you, or taught you to do it for yourself, you might be stuck your whole life thinking ice-cream sandwiches taste like paper.

Amateur teachers and poor writing have contributed to this effect as it regards history. There are few things quite as interesting or tasty as history clearly presented. History is not names and places and dates, although those features are present. History is also not about politics and war and government, although these aspects seem to get a large share of the focus. Rather, history is the consideration of life lived by others, in previous times, in differing circumstances than ourselves, but from the same human perspective. History is the mystery of time, the wonder of others, and the finality and authority of God's laws all mixed together. History is pain and suffering, joy and celebration, and relationships good and bad. History is memory and tradition and lightness and darkness. History is human nature and the rest of nature in juxtaposition. History is a story told in old photographs, a myth told around campfires, the meaning in old-fashioned words. History is real. It happened. And what makes it most interesting; it happened to *them*.

> *"History is the mystery of time, the wonder of others, and the finality and authority of God's laws all mixed together."*

They will always be the most interesting part of it all; the ones before us. They were the ones who lived it first-hand. Our ancient is their modern, our old was their new. Our mystery of history was their reality. Our fictions their truths. I see them in yellowed photographs, staring blankly while holding still for a process that took minutes to our milliseconds. I see them in their writings and their architecture and their art. I see them in their descendents and their creations, and I see them in myself. Each tragedy, each triumph, each dramatic scene, however painted by the sketchiness of the facts that remain to us, each of these were real and vivid to them. They were not better than us, and they were not worse. They were not backwards, and they were not always right. But they do have one thing over us, an advantage we cannot claim until the wheel moves further round its axis, and that is the plain, solid fact that they were *there.*

This is where history comes alive for me. I feel what it might have been like to have been amongst them. I sense their fears and aspirations as they faced events blindly that we see through the advantageous lens of the passing of time. I wonder at their decisions and choices, and yearn to learn from both their failures and triumphs. I stand in awe that God arranged to put them here before me, and wonder why.

I think about *why* we are placed where we are, and *when* we are. And I remember that many of them, an extreme many of them, if I understand the mathematics of the generations properly, were my ancestors. Their blood is pumping through my veins. We have inherited not only the very dirt upon which they trod, but the very tour of duty they have already completed. They have had their turn, and now we have ours. As George Washington said to John Adams at Adams' inauguration, "Now I am fairly out and you are fairly in."

It is our turn, now. Let's see if we can do any better at it than they did. We do have an advantage, after all. We can learn from them. As long as we first take off the wrapper.

A REPUBLIC,
IF YOU CAN KEEP IT

After agonizingly hot summer days spent in argument and compromise, the nearly impossible happened. Delegates from the various states, with different interests, backgrounds, religions, opinions, and constituencies, had agreed on a framework of government. Ratification by each state's legislature was still necessary, and would be no easy task, but the very fact that the Constitution of the United States had been written and agreed to in some form was perhaps the high point in the history of world government.

The story is told of an elderly lady approaching Benjamin Franklin as he emerged from the final session of the Constitutional Convention, at which time she asked him the question, "What sort of government do we have, doctor?" to which he famously answered, "A Republic, if you can keep it."

The United States of America is not a democracy. Ask any school-aged child, and most of his or her parents, however, and they will ape the word "democracy" as though it is the most obvious and pure thing in the world. This is where it is so dangerous that we do not know our history, nor understand our government. The United States of America is MOST CERTAINLY NOT a democracy, and if it ever becomes one, as it has been trending towards for seven decades, it will correspondingly cease to be free. Instead, the United States is a republic. This is a vastly different thing from a democracy, and the distinction is extremely important.

The founders of our country were terrified of democratic rule, a situation in which the masses or majority of men vote for whatever they like in direct assault on the minorities. Protecting minority interests and the rights of the individual was the bedrock upon which the Constitution was founded. The great concern was how to allow a people to be free, how to construct a government "of the people, for the people, by the people," without allowing the passions that grip a people to take over. To do this, the Constitution of the United States, and the accompanying Bill of Rights, established very strong checks and balances and something called The Rule of Law. The Rule of Law is the concept that there are basic freedoms and rights any individual has claim to, and no matter what the desires of the majority or "masses," those individual rights must always be protected. These restrictions, so clearly outlined in those documents, are also meant to bind the government from trampling on the rights of the people, while distributing power across many leaders and branches of government. This concept has worked, and the government of the United States is the oldest government on the planet as a result.

We must get away from the strange belief that whatever the mass of people want is in the country's best interest. U.S. governance is not simply a matter of asking, "What do most of the people want?" as if a poll could indicate righteousness or even pragmatism. Just because a majority of people want something is no indication that it is the right thing to do. This is why it is so important to have a representative government, where the people pick the leaders and give them the power to decide policy according to the Constitution, Bill of Rights, and therefore, the Rule of Law, and not according to the will of the masses. After all, the common man is commonly wrong. Our government and system of laws is there to protect us as much from him as anything or anyone else.

Just why were Franklin's words so prescient that day? Isn't it interesting how he chose to answer the lady's question? Why did he say, "If you can keep it" after telling her it was to be a Republic? Perhaps the wise old statesman knew a thing or two about human nature after all his years as a diplomat, negotiator, and legislator. Perhaps he knew that the temptation would be great for a people to take over their own government and undermine its laws of protection for the individual in the name of interest for selfish interests. Perhaps he could see how the elaborate system of government he'd helped craft could be slowly dismantled over time to serve the masses.

And what of those masses? In the early 1930's Spanish philosopher Jose Ortega y Gasset wrote an instant classic entitled *The Revolt of the Masses,* in which he predicted the doom in Europe that was soon to follow. Ortega coined the term "mass man" to describe the type of person that comprised these waves of the majority; the majority that would vote for its crazy passions, the majority that had employed the guillotine in the French Revolution, the majority that would elect Hitler and the Nazi party to power, the majority that would bring us the Taliban. You see, any time majority rules, individuals suffer. It is the end of freedom. Whenever the "mass man" is given too much power, he always uses it against the individual and those in minority. Ortega said of the mass man:

"Previously, even for the rich and powerful, the world was a place of poverty, difficulty and danger. However rich an individual might be in relation to his fellows, as the world in its totality was poor, the sphere of conveniences and commodities with which his wealth furnished him was very limited. The life of the average man to day is easier, more convenient and safer than that of the most powerful of another age. The common man, finding himself in a world so excellent, technically and socially, believes that it has been produced by nature, and never thinks of the personal efforts of highly-endowed individuals which the creation of this new world presupposed. Still less will he admit the notion that all these facilities still require the support of certain difficult human virtues, the least failure of which would cause the rapid disappearance of the whole magnificent edifice. . . . free expansion of his vital desires . . . his radical ingratitude towards all that has made the ease of his existence . . . the impression that everything is permitted to him and that he has no obligations. . . these spoiled masses are unintelligent enough to believe that the material and social organization, placed at their disposition like the air, is of the same origin, since apparently it never fails them. . . . has caused the masses benefited therby to consider it, not as an organised, but as a natural system . Thus is explained and defined the absurd state of mind revealed by these masses; they are only concerned with their own well-being, and at the same time they remain alien to the cause of that well-being. They imagine their role is limited to demanding these benefits peremptorily, as if they were natural rights."

This is the man of whom Dr. Franklin warned us, then, and this is the man gaining control in the politics of America today. He eats his food, drinks his water, drives on the roads, and consumes everything and anything he wants without ever considering the vast structure of the Rule of Law and the sacrifices of others necessary to set him up so nicely. He does not read, he does not study nor even attempt to understand his history, nor consider the fount of his blessings, and votes accordingly. Placing his vote behind whomever promises to deliver him the most. And in this way, duplicated over millions of such "mass men," a republic slips towards democracy and the desolation that always follows.

"If you can keep it," indeed.

BOOMS, BUST & BALDERDASH - INFLATIONARY BUSINESS CYCLES

If Congress can employ money indefinitely to the general welfare. . . they may appoint teachers in every state. . . The powers of Congress would subvert the very foundation, the very nature of the limited government established by the people of America.
- James Madison

The citizens of any country rely on their political leaders to produce money only in relationship to the wealth of the country. Money cannot be created out of thin air by government fiat. Sure they can print the paper, but the paper has no wealth unless backed by real wealth. Gold, silver and other forms of backing have been used throughout the centuries. A government that would run the paper presses and double their money supply without any real wealth increase from the people has effectively cut the value of all the existing dollars in half.

All the perplexities, confusion and distress in America arise, not from defects in their Constitution or Confederation, not from want of honor or virtue, so much as from the downright ignorance of the nature of coin, credit and circulation.
- John Adams

Imagine owning one unit of stock in a company that has 100 shares and has a net worth of $1000. You own 1% of the value of the company for a $10 stake. Now imagine that the owner prints another 100 shares and sells them on the open market. Someone may pay close to $10 per share through ignorance that the owner produced 100 more shares early in the cycle, but eventually the market will realize that the shares are watered down. The true wealth of the company has not changed overnight, but there are now 200 shares of stock on the market representing the company of a total worth of $1000. This means the effective value of the stock has been cut in half. Your $10 stock has now dropped to $5 after all the buyers learn the full information, in other words, once the market does what markets do. Wealth cannot be created without providing something of value and printing paper is not providing real value. Through no fault of your own, you have lost half the value of your stock because of the company owner's greed. There are protections in place to ensure that this does not happen to your stock, but no protections in place to ensure this doesn't happen to our money supply!

I believe that banking institutions are more dangerous to our liberties than standing armies. Already they have raised up a moneyed aristocracy that has set the government at defiance. The issuing power (of money) should be taken away from the banks and restored to the people to whom it properly belongs.
- Thomas Jefferson

When you save money, you are counting on the "powers that be" to not print more fiat money and destroy the effective value of your hard-earned dollars. But this is exactly what the American government is doing when it produces more money without the financial backing of gold or other real wealth. No other corporations could get away with this type of behavior without major consequences and yet our government does this as a matter of course. Have you felt the pinch of the dollar being less valuable? Have you noticed that in most fields costs are rising precipitously?

The housing bubble is a good example of the analogy I used. Mortgages from our government were flooding the market which means that more dollars were needed to buy the same house. This created an illusion of wealth for people who owned houses, but actually, it was just inflated money that required more of the paper to buy the same house. When people started borrowing against the inflated worth of their house, the bubble was set to burst. The higher housing prices created less demand and less people qualified for the inflated housing prices. What goes up (through fiat money) must come down. When it does, everyone scratches their head and wonders how it all happened.

A nation of well informed men who have been taught to know and prize the rights which God has given them cannot be enslaved. It is in the region of ignorance that tyranny begins.
- Benjamin Franklin

Our government is no longer tied to any standard to regulate how much money is produced. Money should only be produced when the real wealth of the country increases through better productivity. Since the Civil War, money has been slowly freed of the moral restraints imposed by the founding fathers. In the Nixon presidency, our money was completely separated from gold and financial common sense entirely. We now rely on a non-federal cartel of banks to determine our money supply and have a Financial Czar known as the Federal Reserve Chairman who can choose to produce more money at his whim.

What we need is something called "sound money", this is money that is beyond the ability of a government's meddling; a money the people can trust as a proper and changeless representation of the fruit of their labor. Under such money, the government leaders would also have to balance the budget because they would not have fiat money available to print anytime they get into a pinch.

I place economy among the first and most important virtues, and public debt as the greatest of dangers to be feared. To preserve our independence, we must not let our rulers load us with perpetual debt. If we run into such debts, we must be taxed in our meat and drink, in our necessities and in our comforts, in our labor and in our amusements. If we can prevent the government from wasting the labor of the people, under the pretense of caring for them, they will be happy.
- Thomas Jefferson

Ideas shape the course of history - John Maynard Keynes

All great ideas are controversial, or have been at one time - George Seldes

HOW MUCH
CAN WE CARRY?

The average American citizen is like a hiker, and the government a pack upon his back. No hiker can get far without a pack containing key essentials, as no citizen can get far in freedom without a military, police, and the Rule of Law.

Somehow, though, the government keeps convincing the hiker that the pack should be bigger. This slows the hiker, who fights gallantly to grow stronger and still make progress despite the increased burden. Then, the government grows some more and adds more to the pack. The hiker slows further.

Eventually, the hiker is nearly stopped in his forward progress and fights with all he's got to resist toppling over backwards. At this point, slick politicians show up and once again convince the hiker to increase the size of his pack. "To fix your big pack you need to increase it even further."

To accomplish something so incredibly stupid the government has to be very crafty. After all, the pack cannot propell itself, and things can only be added to the pack if the hiker votes it in. So just how does the government convince the hiker to increase his load?

This is where politicians come into the picture. It is their job to get the hiker to add to his own load. To accomplish this, they use many strategies, such as:

1. Envy - if politicians can make the hiker think someone else is carrying a lighter pack than him, he will vote to increase the other peoples' load and decrease his own, assuming that in the process the government will never turn on him.

2. Class Distinction - If the politicians can make the hiker think he is in a group that has an unfair burden compared to someone else, the same trick can be accomplished.

3. Race - Again, if the politician can use any distinction to get the hiker to agree to an increased load for others, Pandora's box is opened and can be used later on everybody.

4. Special Interests - Once again, it's the same old trick. Establish an "us vs. them" situation and promise the "us's" they will benefit at the expense of "them".

5. Misplaced compassion - most people are not educated on the inefficiencies and inconsistencies of government bureaucracy, so they mistakingly think the government can actually execute a social program effectively and thereby "help" people. In other words, politicians know that most people have kind hearts and truly want to make things better, not only for themselves, but for everyone. If the politicians can play to this, they know they will never be held accountable for results because whoever would bring such doubts can be castigated as a "cold-hearted capitalist," or other such name calling which dodges the real question of effectiveness.

6. Misleading or false data - economics and civics can be confusing if misrepresented and argued about enough. The more complicated these subjects can be made to *seem*, the less people will listen to what is actually being said. This is true of almost all areas in which the government doesn't want the public to know what's actually going on. Misconstrued statistics and "expert" opinion can be used to "prove" almost any position. Eventually, the people will vote for a talking head that produces good sound bites and looks and acts the part. Don't be fooled: self-assuredness is no proof of competence.

There are more than just what's represented in this short list, but the flavor for all of them is the same: make the hiker think it is in his own best interest to increase his load, then get him to blame anything except the heavy burden on his back for his faltering progress!

Even more incredible is the ability of politicians to not only get the hiker to miss the obvious problem of the governmental burden on his back, but they even succeed in getting the hiker to blame the freedom he has to hike along the trail! Economist and investor Peter Schiff says it best:

"What worries me most, however, is the almost automatic backlash that attributes the present economic collapse to a failure of capitalism and free-market economics and turns it into an argument for expanded government. Never mind that government created a crisis that the free market would have avoided altogether . . . ."

Here is what politicians have convinced the hiker to allow to be done to himself:

1. Escalating taxes (WAY over 50% when taken as a whole)
2. Government deficit spending (meaning, on a yearly basis, the government spends BILLIONS more than it takes in)
3. Exponential growth in national debt (yearly deficits added together, year after year, compounded by interest)
4. Skyrocketing unfunded debt (Social Security, etc.)
5. Massive international trade imbalance
6. Inflationary monetary policies (Inflation means the government prints more money and adds it to the money supply already out there. This makes prices of everything go up and the money you have less valuable. This is the government's favorite tax, because it doesn't have to voted on, is not understood by many, can be easily hidden, and helps reduce the problem of the growing national debt because the amount owed shrinks in value with a declining dollar.) Remember this: our government actualy loves inflation, needs inflation, and misrepre-

sents just how big inflation is annually so people won't understand what is taking place with their hard-earned savings.

7. Swelling government bureaucracy (the unelected portion of our government, which barely existed a hundred years ago, now is a behemoth impossible to quantify financially or politically)

8. Enormous foreign aid grants (and now we've just decided to pay for abortions in other countries with U.S. tax dollars)

9. Military operations almost everywhere around the globe

10. Increasing "welfare" society of government social programs

Any hiker that thinks he needs a heavier pack to make it easier for him to walk simply does not understand how the world works.

We have a choice.

We can elect government officials who will gut our government, or our government will gut us. Either we put some government employees out of work to save the people, or we will see most of the people work to feed the government.

Make no mistake about it: the pack can't increase indefinitely. Some day, at some point, the hiker will topple over backwards.

Then what?

Let's hope the hiker does what any intelligent traveler would do: start chucking the dead weight before it's too late!

He that would make his own liberty secure, must guard even his enemy from opposition; for if he violates this duty he establishes a precedent that will reach himself. - Thomas Paine

History does not teach fatalism. There are moments when the will of a handful of free men breaks through determinism and opens up new roads. - Charles de Gaulle

Freedom has its life in the hearts, the actions, the spirit of men and so it must be daily earned and refreshed - else like a flower cut from its life-giving roots, it will wither and die.
- Dwight D. Eisenhower

I prefer liberty with danger to peace with slavery.
- Author Unknown

Liberty means responsibility. That is why most men dread it.
- George Bernard Shaw

The people never give up their liberties but under some delusion. - Edmund Burke

LIVE WHILE
YOU'RE ALIVE

Life is a gift. Each day is precious. We have all been born with talents and abilities and a purpose to serve. But life is also deceptively easy to squander. We waste a few minutes and then notice that days have slipped by. We count down the time to leave work at the end of a day and then watch our weekend blaze by. We say yes to a lot of things that aren't really aligned with our highest purposes in life and give away our time too cheaply.

We have clocks in our cars, on our hands, on our walls, and on our computers, but we always seem to be out of time. We rush and hurry and scurry about but never really seem to get much accomplished. We keep telling ourselves that we will slow things down, live our priorities, and make time for the important things as soon as. . . .

That phrase, "as soon as," has enabled the slaughter of thousands of precious hours of our lives. We use it to escape from the fact that we aren't really doing all our dreams and purpose require of us, but "as soon as" reassures us that we will "some day" and keeps us wasting time.

Then, at some imperceptible point along the way, "as soon as" becomes "if only I would have." We see more in our past than we do in our future. We begin feeling as if it's too late. We start thinking we've blown our chance to live the life we always felt, deep down inside, that we should, that we could, and that we *What makes you come alive?* would. But time doesn't stand still. It waits for no man. It rushes by us unmercifully. "Some day" never comes.

What makes you come alive? What do you feel deep inside that you can and should do with your time? What is your great purpose, aligned with your obvious abilities, that God has planted within you?

In the words of William Wallace in the movie *Braveheart*, "Every man dies, not every man really lives." May that statement not be true of you. May you live while you're alive!

A positive attitude may not solve all your problems, but it will annoy enough people to make it worth the effort.
- Herm Albright

Attitudes are contagious. Are yours worth catching?
- Dennis and Wendy Mannering

Wherever you go, no matter what the weather, always bring your own sunshine. - Anthony J. D'Angelo

GET HISTORY
WITH PEOPLE

Leaders must learn to build relationships. It is through relationships that we are able to influence others, be influenced ourselves, and receive some of life's richest blessings. The relationships in your life should be some of your most prized "possessions."

One of the things I have always tried to teach about building relationships is to get history with people. This means spending time with them and experiencing the things that life throws at us, together. Sometimes this will involve funny occurrences, strange events, memorable experiences, or touching moments. There is little substitute for time spent together. Time allows shared experiences. Those shared experiences build bonds and create lasting connections. Think back through your life and the relationships that have mattered. Weren't there special memories and fun times that marked those relationships in your life?

People can be challenging, prickly, annoying, and grating. But they can also be enjoyable, fun, inspiring, and warm. Choose carefully the type of people with whom you'd like to spend the days of your life. Look for those who reciprocate your warmth, positive attitude, and beliefs. Look for those who will lift you, encourage you, stand by you, and contribute to your life. Then find ways to spend time together, letting the things happen that will happen. Be intentional about the building of relationships in your life. Contribute to others, be an up-lifter and a good-finder. Ask yourself if you are the kind of friend a friend would like to have. Be there when needed. Keep promises. Find little ways

Choose carefully the type of people with whom you'd like to spend the days of your life.

35

to be an enhancer in the lives of others. Do all these things and I promise that you will not only have some of the best campfire stories to tell at the end of your days, but there will be many people there who'll want to hear them!

> *Early in life, I decided that I would not be overcome by events. My philosophy has been that regardless of the circumstances, I shall not be vanquished, but will try to be happy. Life is not easy for any of us. But it is a continual challenge, and it is up to us to be cheerful - and to be strong, so that those who depend on us may draw strength from our example.* - Rose Kennedy

BURGOYNE'S PROCLAMATION

In June of 1777, flamboyant General "Gentleman Johnny" Burgoyne initiated his attack on the colonies from Canada. He commanded over seven thousand infantrymen, a combination of British redcoats and Hessian mercenaries, a small army of artillery specialists and 138 cannon, four hundred Native Americans, and some Canadians and colonial Tories.

Burgoyne was not satisfied with the attacking power of his military force, however, for in addition to it he let loose a barrage of negative press. Chief among his efforts was a proclamation issued on June 23 in which Burgoyne "accused the leaders of the 'unnatural Rebellion' of perpetrating 'Arbitrary Imprisonments, Confiscation of Property, Persecution and Torture . . . without Distinction of Age or Sex, for the sole Crime . . . of having adhered in Principle to the Government under which they were born. And if the 'Phrenzy and Hostility should remain, I trust I shall stand acquitted in the Eyes of God and Men in denouncing and executing the Vengeance of the State against the willful Outcast.'"

Despite his blowhard style, the threats and the condemnations, despite his bragging that he could command the "Vengeance of the State," Burgoyne was utterly defeated and ended up surrendering his entire army. He failed on many accounts, and he was aided in his failure by the decision of General Howe not to march to his aid. Although Burgoyne is generally acclaimed as a decent soldier, historians are largely in agreement that he was not a good leader. His arrogance and self-assuredness on topics in which he was not an expert (though he assumed himself to be), were the seeds of his undoing. Burgoyne totally underestimated the time and toil

37

required to march a large army through the wilderness, and he missed entirely the strategies of battles in the woods and hills. He also failed to properly grasp the complexities of dealing with his Native American allies, and this was partly responsible for their desertion of him at an inopportune moment. Finally, Burgoyne made a beginner's mistake and violated the basic rule of engagement to never divide one's force in the face of an enemy, and split his into three.

Although bold, brave and extremely perseverant, Burgoyne's weaknesses were too great to overcome. He lead a brave fight, but cost England dearly. The combination of Howe's refusal to coordinate strategy with Burgoyne's attack and Burgoyne's own mistakes and false assumptions resulted in an enormous defeat that shocked Europe. The timely news resulted in increased French involvement in the colonial cause, and a continuing drain on resources and supplies for the English.

Reading Burgoyne's proclamation of June 23 is almost laughable in hindsight.

The pages of history are littered with individuals who assumed too much about their own competence and then cost their causes, companies, or armies enormously as a result. But great leaders are humble creatures. They "know that they don't know," and they spend their lives learning and growing and asking and seeking. Great leaders are slow to beat their chests and slow to threaten. Great leaders are all about love, caring, compassion, commitment, and cause. In the words of theologian Stuart W. Scott, "The qualities that one must strongly possess in order to carry out a leadership role are wisdom, initiative, decisiveness, humility, courage, and personal involvement." Try to imagine an effective leader who is deficient in even one of these categories. Impossible. In the case of Burgoyne in the wilderness, he was strongly lacking in two: humility and wisdom. Curiously, he was quite certain of his own wisdom, thereby failing in the humility category. This was his and his army's undoing. And ultimately, it lead to the failure of England's iron-fisted rule in the colonies.

Leadership matters!

FOUNDATIONS OF FREEDOM
PART I

I was asked to expand upon reference I made in a recent talk about the trail of writings that lead to the founding documents of the United States. To begin the discussion, I want to borrow an excellent graphic from W. Cleon Skousen, the founder of the National Center for Constitutional Studies (see *A Miracle That Changed the World: The 5000 Year Leap*). At the extreme left end of the scale is 100% Tyranny and what is called "Ruler's Law." At the extreme right end of the scale is 100% Anarchy and is called "No Law." According to Skousen, somewhere in the middle is the sweet spot and is called "People's Law."

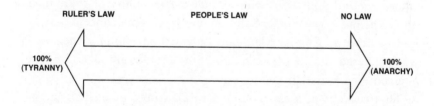

It is this People's Law that the founders of the United States enshrined in the Constitution to defend the people from oppressive government while at the same time protecting them from each other. Communism and fascism, although sometimes confused as being extremes from opposite ends (one at the extreme "left," the other at the extreme "right"), are actually different names for the same thing: tyranny. They both involve police state control of people's lives. Dictators, Marxists, redistributionists, and Islamic Theocracies all live at this extreme end of the spectrum. Ultimately, the "Ruler's Law" extreme involves control of the people by force for the benefit of the state.

Anarchy and chaos live at the other extreme, where there is no law whatsoever. While this may at first seem to be the purest form of freedom, it takes only a little consideration to see that when everyone is free to behave entirely as they like, nobody is free. This is because everyone's freedoms infringe upon each other.

To officially establish a government in the middle of the two extremes, the founders of the United States drew upon the writings and philosophies of a great many minds. Interestingly, given the very similar style of "classical education" most of the founders received (see *American Creation*, by Joseph J. Ellis) the founders had similar backgrounds in classical literature. (It is a shame that this has virtually disappeared in our society today). This produced a collective knowledge that facilitated extremely well-informed debate, and ultimately resulted in the most incredible and unique creation of a government, by the people, for the people, the world had ever seen.

The basis for People's Law can be traced back to the original Anglo Saxons which began occupying the island of England somewhere around 450 A.D., who in turn based many of their ideas upon ancient Israel (before the monarchy). This concept became known later as English Common Law: called *common* because it was assumed that it was commonly understood by all to be true, and commonly distributed to all.

This concept of a law common to all came, in part, from the writings of the Roman lawyer and statesman, Cicero. According to Skousen, Cicero expounded upon " . . . the brilliant intelligence of a supreme Designer with an ongoing interest in both human and cosmic affairs. Cicero's compelling honesty led him to conclude that once the reality of the Creator is clearly identified in the mind, the only intelligent approach to government, justice, and human relations is in terms of the laws which the Supreme Creator has already established. The Creator's order of things is called Natural Law." In the words of Cicero himself (Quoted in Ebenstein, *Great Political Thinkers*, p. 133),

"True Law is right reason in agreement with nature, it is of universal application, unchanging and everlasting; it summons to duty by its commands, and averts from wrongdoing by its prohibitions .. .. It is a sin to try to alter this law, nor is it allowable to repeal any part of it, and it is impossible to abolish it entirely. We cannot be freed from its obligations by senate or people, and we need not look outside ourselves for an expounder or interpreter of it. And there will not be different laws at Rome and at Athens, or different laws now and in the future, but one eternal and unchangeable law will be valid for all nations and all times, and there will be one master and ruler, that is God, over us all, for he is the author of this law, its promulgator, and its enforcing judge. Whoever is disobedient is fleeing from himself and denying his human nature, and by reason of this very fact he will suffer the worst punishment."

Cicero concluded that man must rid himself of the depravity that came from relying upon himself, and should instead return to reliance upon "Natural Law." In effect, Cicero predicated that all law should be measured against God's Law.

The founding fathers of the United States established their new government upon the foundation of Natural Law, summoning harmony with the law's of "Nature's God." How sad that our citizenry have forgotten this great truth.

THE CURSE OF
WEALTH UNEARNED

Whenever modern situations become worrisome it is nearly always instructive to peer back into history for perspective and understanding. With the crazy, off-the-wall economic policies of the current United States government, there are many historical events from which one can draw context. One such moment is the monarchy of Spain during the 1500s. See for yourself if there are not many parallels.

In the late 1400's, explorations for gold and passages to the east produced the discovery of what became known as the New World. Spain quickly edged out Portugal as the dominant player in this game throughout much of the 1500s, and literally tons of gold and silver made its way across the Atlantic from the infamous Spanish Main in Mexico, Latin and South America to the coffers in Seville, Spain. There were many unfortunate effects of this, such as the near total decimation of the Inca and Mayan native populations, as well as the instigation of the African slave trade. First the natives, and increasingly so the Africans, were needed to man the mines. As a result of this system, massive amounts of gold and silver were hauled across the Atlantic and into Europe. Some estimates say that this amount was so enormous that the total amount of precious metal in Europe at the end of the 1500s was more than five times what it was at the beginning of that century when the New World was discovered!

It would be logical to deduce that Spain became one of the richest nations in the world as a result of this massive influx of stolen treasure. But interestingly, and very educationally, this was not the case.

What happened?

Author Peter L. Bernstein writes:

"Once the gold began arriving in quantity, the Spanish were far more proficient at spending than at producing. The massive imports of gold and silver stimulated the spending skills at the same time that they stifled Spain's incentive to produce. Spain acted like a poor man who makes a great windfall at the gambling tables but comes to believe that the money is his destiny rather than a nonrecurring event . . . . Late in the century the . . . Parliament declared, 'The more of [gold] that comes in, the less the Kingdom has. . . Though our kingdoms should be the richest in the world . . . they are the poorest, for they are only a bridge for [the gold and silver] to go to the Kingdoms of our enemies.' Another Spanish observer, Pedro de Valencia, wrote, 'So much silver and money . . . always has been fatal poison to republics and cities. They believe money will keep them and it is not true: plowed fields, pastures, and fisheries are what give sustenance.' Gold has always been associated with power. Once the kings of Spain realized how much new wealth the discoveries of gold in the American colonies would bring them, they convinced themselves that their wealth was great enough to bend the world to their will.'"

An apt analogy would be of 'second generation wealth.' It is almost a cliché that sons squander their father's wealth, thinking that they have somehow, by eating at the same table, sleeping under the same roof, and being sufficiently 'talked at' by the patriarch, been bestowed the 'magic touch' which their father used to produce the wealth in the first place. The squandering of the father's empire in such cases is so common as to be almost a rule. This is because there is no 'touch' of greatness, or family superiority, nor endowments or bestowed rights, there are only the laws of success. And those laws are almost immediately broken by a son taking over the reigns of a great empire for which he was not forced to labor to create nor strive to earn. The violation of the earning principle produces harsh results and even harsher lessons. Sorry golden boys.

Another comparison, and the one that inspired this article, is made to the current United States government and its hubris and arrogance in thinking it has found its own Spanish Main in the printing of free money by the Federal Reserve banking scam (er, um, I mean banking system). Having arranged for itself a tidy little situation in which it can produce currency out of nothing, the government has taken to acting like the monarch of sixteenth century Spain, with figurative ships laden with "bailout money" and "earmarks." Our bureaucratic government has taken leave of its senses in a 'gold fever' all its own creation, thinking it can disdain major industrial and agricultural infrastructures while gifting billions of dollars in bailouts to its partners in banking complicit in its schemes. Worse, it seems to think it can foist this on an American citizenry without ramifications, as though Americans are naive Incas or backward Mayans.

Tellingly, however, the Incas were not naïve; but merely trusting. The Mayans were not backwards: but only fooled into thinking the Spaniards were gods. Today, Americans, or at least some of them, seem to be falling into the same traps of the Incas and the Mayans: too trusting of the government, and somehow duped into believing in political messiahs. To continue such foolishness will result in the same fate as the indigenous peoples of Latin and South America: decimation.

"Consumption is made possible by production and credit is made possible by savings."
- Peter Schiff

But America cannot stand upon its stolen spending power any more than Spain could stand upon its stolen treasure. Wealth unearned bears with it a curse. Instead, as Peter Schiff said, "Consumption is made possible by production and credit is made possible by savings." Government economic shenanigans are no substitute, but rather a drug taken to defer the pain until later, at which time the pain is even greater.

TYRANNY FALLS

I recently read a great article from Steven Hayward entitled *The Berlin Wall Ten Years Later,* published by the Ashbrook Center. It is incredible to me that tyrants genuinely believe they can keep a group of people against their will in a tyrannical system. Any cursory glance at history would clearly prove the illusory nature and long term unenforceability of any tyrannical scheme. It takes one's breath away that tyrants would believe they can deny the people their freedom and not suffer the consequences all tyrants eventually must face. Here is the article with my comments on the philosophy of oppression and captivity interested after each paragraph.

Ten years ago this week the Berlin Wall started to come down, and it was immediately evident that the Communist empire would come down with it. A few years before the Berlin Wall went up in 1961, the Russian writer Ilya Ehrenburg offered what would become a fitting epitaph for Communist tyranny: "If the whole world were to be covered with asphalt, one day a crack would appear in that asphalt; and in that crack, grass would grow." The crack in the Wall in 1989 proved to be the fatal fissure.

Tyranny can only survive by threats, intimidation, and by blocking the free movement of people, ideas, and money.

Tyranny is based upon lies and when the lies are called lies by the courageous people the end is near. Tyranny relies on the masses of people to sit by quietly and allow the walls to be built up around them.

When President Ronald Reagan went to Berlin in 1987 and s aid "Mr. Gorbachev, tear down this wall" (a line his foreign policy advisers tried several times to delete from his speech), most observers thought, "There he goes again." Reagan had predicted back in 1983 that it would be Communism, not western democracy, that would end up on the ash heap of history. Almost no one thought the beginning of the end would come before the decade was over. How did Reagan know?

Leaders are typically criticized for standing up to tyranny. Many managers think a program of détente with tyranny is acceptable. True leaders know that détente with tyranny enslaves people in an unnatural system that denies people their God-given rights. President Ronald Reagan courageously called the Communist system what it was: a Godless materialistic system that denies people their freedoms and humanity. Reagan understood that tyranny only survives by counting on the passivity of the masses. Reagan awoke the masses to the hope of a better tomorrow!

One other modern statesman predicted the demise of communism before the century's end—Winston Churchill. In the mid-1950s, when Churchill was Prime Minister for the second time, he told a young aide that if he lived his normal span of life he would surely see Eastern Europe free from Communism. How did Churchill know?

Winston Churchill understood the lies of communism also. He knew that any system that denies people the right to freely choose their futures is tyranny, no matter how much it is justified by propaganda. Human freedom is a God-given right. If the freedoms are taken from the people, then any leader with a historical perspective will know it is temporary. Tyranny is a system that forces people to do what the managers say, regardless of the people's desires.

Reagan and Churchill came to their assurance about the fate of Communism by the simple recognition that a social system so wholly unnatural could not long endure, even with the powerful sci-

entific props of modern tyranny. The Berlin Wall was the ultimate artifact of this unnatural system: unlike the Great Wall of China or other bastions, the Berlin Wall was the first bulwark intended to keep people in instead of out. Reagan had noticed the significance of this back in the early 1960s, and his resolve was bolstered by a visit he made to East Berlin before he was president, during which, his traveling companions said, Reagan shook with rage at the tyranny he saw first hand. He resolved that "We must do something to free these people."

Walls are typically built to keep invaders out, but tyranny builds walls to keep people in! Tyrants however, will claim the wall is to keep people out; exactly what the East German government did. They claimed the wall was to keep the West Germans out of East Germany and told the lie repeatedly to their constituents. Reagan could not believe the hubris of the East German communist government. What kind of system would force people to stay in a system against their will and lie about the purpose of the wall? Any courageous leader would resolve to do something to free the people from the Godless tyranny. What type of leader would continue to allow the people to suffer while they benefited by the loss of freedom for others? Reagan vowed to do something about this! The world has benefited from his courage and resolve.

As Churchill contemplated at the end of World War II the division of Europe that would necessarily come with Soviet occupation of the East, he remarked to Charles de Gaulle that while the Soviets were a hungry wolf now, "after the meal come the digestion period," and that the Soviet Union would not be able to digest the peoples of Eastern Europe. Sure enough, every few years, like a burp of indigestion, a part of Eastern Europe would flare up and require to be put down forcibly—Hungary in 1956; Czechoslovakia in 1968; Poland in 1981.

Tyranny is not capable of maintaining its power base. Tyrants may implement a tyrannical system, but the people will eventually wake up to their plight. They will throw the tyrants out of power and give freedom back to the people. In every system based on tyranny there is a history of revolts and flare ups. This is a sign that the people are dissatisfied and will eventually overcome the tyrants. Each revolt builds in power and resolve until the innate dream for freedom cannot be held back.

By early 1989 it was time for another period of Eastern European indigestion. It was no longer possible for the Soviet Union to check the desire of Eastern Europeans to be free. A military crackdown would have made a hash of Gorbachev's program of glasnost ("openness") and perestroika ("restructuring") and ruined Soviet-American relations at a crucial time.

Repeated waves of resistance to tyranny and lack of results in the communist systems eventually produces change. It becomes no longer possible for the tyranny to resist the desire of the people to be free. A forceful crackdown on the aspirations of the people makes a mockery of the alleged slogans and value system of the tyranny. Tyranny is always hypocritical, claiming freedoms and independence to the people while building walls and ruling with fear and intimidation.

The beginning of the end started in Hungary. After Solidarity had swept an election in Poland, reformers within the Hungarian ruling Communist party pushed for a genuine multi-party election there as well. A divided Communist party was unable to blunt the momentum for a process that it knew was likely to be its death sentence. But reformers knew that they faced great hazards during the transitional phase, and they feared that another 1956-style military crackdown might be in store, perhaps from East Germany (whose Stalinist leadership never did sympathize with Gorbachev's program) if not the Soviet Union.

Tyranny is a house of cards and will fall when freedom-loving people act with courage. The more light that shines into the hypocritical behavior of the tyrants, the faster tyranny will fall. The reformers know they will be subject to attacks through the press, judicial system, police, etc, but continue the course because they know the truth and history are on their side.

So the Hungarians decided on a bold stroke. They opened their border with Austria, and stopped detaining East Germans who transited through Hungary en route to Austria. A back door around the Berlin Wall had opened up, and thousands were pouring through. The Hungarians did not inform the Soviet Union or East Germany in advance. "We were pretty sure," Hungarian reformer Imre Pozsgay said later, "that if hundreds of thousands of East Germans went to the West, the East German regime would fall, and in that case Czechoslovakia was also out."

The Hungarians opened their border with Austria and people departed by the millions. They did not need to be solicited by the Austrians, but left freely when given the choice. This is the fatal flaw in every tyrannical system—the majority of the people will choose freedom over tyranny and will leave if given a choice. Communism fell—not from an outside attack—but from the internal rot.

They were right. Throughout the fall protests in East German cities were growing, reaching a climax on November 4, when a million people took to the streets of East Berlin. East Germany's aging tyrant, Erich Honecker, had stepped down in October, but it was too late. His successors bowed to the inevitable on November 9, and announced the opening of the borders to the West. Within hours thousands of Germans from both sides of the Berlin divide descended on the Wall with picks and hammers. "We did not suspect," the East German foreign minister wrote, "that the opening of the Wall was the beginning of the end of the Republic." He was clearly oblivious to Ehrenburg's prophecy that once a blade of grass poked through the concrete, the Wall would come tumbling down.

When enough people rise up against tyrannical masters the system of oppression will fall. More than a million people took to the streets and in the end the wall tumbled down—just as Reagan and

Churchill said it would. The tyrants had no idea how many people hated their regime and how quickly it would be discarded when given a choice. A free people will choose freedom and opportunity over oppression and slavery every time. Ronald Reagan said it best, "Mr. Gorbachev, Tear down this wall!" As the Bible says, "The Truth will set you free."

The patriot's blood is the seed of Freedom's tree.
- Thomas Campbell

Here is my advice as we begin the century that will lead to 2081. First, guard the freedom of ideas at all costs. Be alert that dictators have always played on the natural human tendency to blame others and to oversimplify. And don't regard yourself as a guardian of freedom unless you respect and preserve the rights of people you disagree with to free, public, unhampered expression. - Gerard K. O'Neill

Those who deny freedom to others deserve it not for themselves.
- Abraham Lincoln

Freedom is never free. - Author Unknown

Many politicians are in the habit of laying it down as a self-evident proposition that no people ought to be free till they are fit to use their freedom. The maxim is worthy of the fool in the old story who resolved not to go into the water till he had learned to swim. - Thomas Macaulay

Where the Spirit of the Lord is, there is liberty.
- Holy Bible

ENCOURAGING IN A DISCOURAGING WORLD

The longer I lead people, the more I am convinced that encouragement is the number one thing a leader gives. Developing a vision, developing a plan, setting goals, etc. are all important, but none of these will work without the power of encouragement. I have been blessed with a mentor that has encouraged me to grow. Pastor Robert L. Dickie has always seen the potential in me and made me want to live up to that potential. I have in turn focused on the potential in others and encouraged them to live up to it as well. As a leader, I will continue to lead with or without the encouragement, but encouragement sure makes the road smoother. I have seen people blossom under encouragement that were faltering under discouragement. No one can make you successful in life, but encouragement is like the oil in a race engine. No matter how well designed the engine, if it's not oiled properly, it will overheat and burn out. Find people in your life who can pour cooling oil on your overheating engine, then do the same for them.

The people close to you need to hear that you believe in them. They need to know that you love them and are willing to sacrifice for them. All of us get poured on by the negative media, negative people, and hypocritical actions of others, but we must choose to be the light for others. Are you a light in other people's lives? Are you the person that people see to be uplifted? Outside of character, encouragement is the number one trait that I would pray every person develops. I am proud of you for being the light to others in a dark world. One person can make a difference. Be the difference that you long to see in the world and never be weary in well doing!

One person can make a difference!

PUTTING GAS IN YOUR TANK

This discussion is designed to make you think. I am going to share some of my personal story today. This is not done to make you believe the way I believe, but to help you understand the process that ideas have on your thought life. Please think through your own beliefs and convictions as you are reading about mine. My goal is to help you think better by understanding the power that ideas have to change lives. I like to review my core beliefs every year to ensure that my beliefs are corresponding with the world that I am living in. I think this is a good thinking habit for all of us to practice.

I have talked about how encouragement is the oil to keep the engine of a leader cool. Today, let's talk about the gas that powers the engine. Human beings act on the ideas contemplated in their minds. Better ideas lead to better actions, just as better gas leads to better performance in an engine. I have had a couple of breakthrough years that led to better thinking. 1993 was a groundbreaking year for me, because I learned better ideas lead to better results. I read extensively on personal development and improved my outer results greatly. Outside, I was achieving great results, but inside I was miserable and unhappy. 1997 was another groundbreaking year. This was the year that I truly surrendered to Jesus Christ. Until then, I had my will and I thought I had added Jesus to my team on a part-time basis. After 1997, I realized it was His team and my part was to do His will on earth full-time. This was major idea shift indeed! When it was my team, the roadblocks and setbacks stopped me because I was never sure that the price was worth the reward. When I joined Christ's team, I no longer doubted that any price is worth the reward – even if the rewards were not on earth.

Think about the gas that you are pouring into your tank. Are you beset by doubts and fears? My good friend Tim Marks says, "Know why you believe what you believe." Every great achiever is a believer in something bigger than himself. Protagoras said, "Man is the measure of all things." This was my philosophy for several years and I found man to be too small a measurement. If man is the measurement of all things, then there are no absolutes that relate to all men. Each man will set his own measurements. If there are no absolutes, then there are no convictions that relate to all mankind. If there are no convictions, then courage is weakened. Less courage leads to less leadership. A leader leads with the courage of his convictions and people follow those with convictions. I say all of this to ask a few questions. What are your convictions? What principles do you feel so strongly about that you would suffer for them? Are you willing to die for your convictions? In our post-modern world, few people have convictions worth dying for.

Patrick Henry's famous statement, "Give me liberty or give me death," rings hollow in today's relative world. We can laugh at Mr. Henry or we can ask what beliefs gave him the courage to stand against the overwhelming force of England and King George. No one who reads history can doubt that the founding fathers had beliefs that were non-negotiable. No one doubts that they were not perfect and fell

> *"Give me liberty or give me death."*
> - Patrick Henry

short of their ideals, but at least they had ideals. What concerns me about the daily buffet of post-modern ideas is the glorification of the cynic over the courageous person. Please tell me what countries erect statues in the main square to the cynic who said it couldn't be done? Or to the cynic who said it isn't worth doing? Only someone who is fixated on themselves (man being the measure) could say that. Anyone with the courage of his convictions and focused on the welfare (economic, political, and spiritual) of others would never say striving isn't worth it. When you are setting your goals for your future, I would encourage you begin with the end in mind. Start with your core beliefs and convictions. Why do you believe what you believe? What are the long-term results for believing this? Do these beliefs lead to a world-view that accurately describes the world we live in? The closer your world-view accurately describes reality, the better you will do at living in the world.

So fill your tanks, from a correct world-view, with productive thoughts. If your focus is correct, you'll understand that greatness is worth the struggle.

If you don't get everything you want, think of the things you don't get that you don't want. - Oscar Wilde

If you don't think every day is a good day, just try missing one. - Cavett Robert

Oh, my friend, it's not what they take away from you that counts. It's what you do with what you have left. - Hubert Humphrey

THE EDUCATION
OF A LEADER

Author Richard Brookheiser wrote, "There is no formula for educating a leader, because he must be responsible for much of his own education himself."

One of the top priorities for any leader is education. The formal variety may be fine, but the type of education to which I'm referring encompasses much more than that. It begins with the spirit of gaining knowledge. Leaders and would-be leaders alike must be hungry for learning, and the result should be habitual, ongoing, aggressive, self-education.

It is the job of the leader, and no one else, to advance his own education. Leaders learn from many sources and circumstances. Here is just a short list:

1. Other leaders: Leaders learn from others; those who provide a good example and those who provide a bad one. Leaders should always look at those who've gone before them in a category, endeavor, or situation and seek to glean what can be useful from that person's experience. As the saying goes, experience is the best teacher: OTHER people's experience!

2. Mentors: One of the lost arts of leadership is the use of a mentor. Many of the great leaders throughout history had excellent mentors for at least portions of their lives. Mentors can provide clarity, insight, and guidance in areas of blindness or ignorance for the leader. Friends will tell you what you want to hear, mentors will tell you what you need to hear. It may not always be comfortable, you might not always want to hear what the mentor has to say, but a true leader will want to

55

know the truth so he or she can become more effective.

3. Experience: It has been joked that experience comes from good judgment. And good judgment occurs after enough bad judgment. In other words, experience is a trial and error affair. The only way to process our mistakes productively is to learn from them and never repeat them. It's okay to make a mistake, but it's never okay to continue on with that same mistake, and certainly not to the point where the mistake becomes a destructive habit. Our experiences are there to make us better. Take all you can from each one, and bend it into an education.

4. Books: Almost without exception the great leaders of the ages have been big readers. However, most people don't read, and of those that do, most of them are reading only for entertainment. Leaders, on the contrary, read with a specific intent to get better, to gain insight, and to grow in wisdom, discernment, and influence. Richard Brookhiser, in his excellent book *George Washington on Leadership* wrote, "Washington supplemented a meager education with a lifetime of self-education. Washington would read history, and military history, all his life."

These are just four of the methods leaders have to learn the principles and specifics of their trade. The key is that the education of a leaders becomes a magnificent obsession. It should be developed as the most precious professional skill. When a leader is through learning, he or she is through!

What habits are you forming in the area of personal development? Are you hungry for learning? Are you reading good books on a regular basis? Do you have a mentor? Do you organize your experiences and/or thoughts in a journal or in "game planning" sessions? Are you "thinking ahead of the airplane" or just taking the shots of life as they come? Are you associating with other leaders?

May the goal of all your learning not be knowledge, but action!

ACTIONS ACCUMULATE - CAESAR AUGUSTUS

Gaius Octavius was born in 63 B.C.. Nephew to acting dictator of Rome, Julius Caesar, Gaius was (unbeknownst to anyone until after Caesar's death) named Caesar's adopted son and heir. Only eighteen years old at that time, he was instantly a wealthy man, and had the additional clout of his adopted father's name. In ancient Rome, however, this was not enough. The country was not yet run as a dynastic empire, and birth was no guarantee of ascent to power. Competing factions in the senate and former advisors and consuls to Rome jockeyed for position. Nobody gave the young teenager much credit, and few would have predicted his determined rise to power. Eventually, however, Gaius Octavius, later known as Caesar Augustus (for which the month of August is named), became Rome's first and longest ruling emperor. His efforts effectively killed the last remnants of Republican Rome and ushered in the approximately five-hundred year Age of Empire. The story of his patient, brilliant, and ruthless rise to his position as the most powerful man in the world is gripping and as racy as a soap opera. Leadership lessons abound in his long and storied career.

One prominent feature of Augustus's life is his incredible ability to hold the long-term view of things. While others sought short term fixes, Octavius was patient enough to maneuver for long-term solutions. Opposed by powerful and ruthless men (and treacherous women working behind the scenes), Augustus was able to take one step at a time, carefully and deliberately, until he was literally the last man standing in the quest for power.

Perhaps the biggest thing a leader can learn from the life of one of the world's most successful leaders is Augustus's ability to compound the effects of his actions over a long period of time. Augustus had the rare ability to pile one forward move on top of another, and spent very little time doing what most average men do: wasting their lives re-doing the same things over and over again. Augustus rarely squandered a resource or opportunity, and used every advance as a stepping off point for another. Most people do not operate this way. Power-thirst and ruthlessness aside, Augustus is a great example of a leader's efficient, cumulative use of time and resources.

Our money, our time, our relationships, our connections, our reputation, our name, our education, and our abilities are all assets that can help us advance throughout our lives. Sadly, however, many of us waste and squander much of this "capital" along the way. We blow our money, sabotage our relationships, deconstruct our credibility, tarnish our name, refuse to continue or utilize our educations, and fail to manage and cultivate our connections. In so doing we find ourselves having to cover the same ground again and again. We have to earn money to replace that which we spent so unwisely. We seek new relationships because we haven't been able to sustain or grow the old ones. We make new connections because people have stopped trusting us. We are forced to learn the same lessons over and over again. In short, we start over again and again. This is like an army that charges up a hill and successfully pushes the enemy off, only to endure a self-inflicted retreat back down to charge that same hill once again! As Orrin Woodward says, "Some people who have been doing something for thirty years with little to show for it cannot claim they have thirty years of experience. They have one year of experience thirty times!"

The best leaders leverage all that they have to get everything they want.

The best leaders leverage all that they have to get everything they want. This requires a long term view, a respect for the assets in their possession, and the ability to keep from sabotaging their own progress. Life is too short to learn the same lessons over and over again, or to re-do what has previously been done. Consistency is also crucial. Effort upon effort, consistently applied over time, produces tremendous compound results. Conversely, inconsistency is one of life's supreme inefficiencies.

In the end, success is largely a matter of hanging on after others have been shaken off. It is also the accumulation of consistent effort over time. The best leaders build an edifice out of their lives, taking steps each day to add to previous accomplishments. The rest struggle in futile repeats. We only get one life. The choice is ours.

FOUNDATIONS OF FREEDOM
PART II

If Cicero provided the foundation that there is a concept of Natural Law delivered by the hand of a Natural Law Giver, then others expounded upon what rights are inherit under that law. One among these is the Englishman, John Locke. Locke wrote:

"The state of Nature has a law of Nature to govern it, which . . . teaches all mankind who will but consult it, that being all equal and independent, no one ought to harm another in his life, health, liberty or possessions; for men being all the workmanship of one omnipotent and infinitely wise maker; all the servants of one sovereign master, sent into the world by His order and about His business; they are His property . . .And, being furnished with like faculties, sharing all in one community of Nature, there cannot be supposed any such subordination among us that may authorize us to destroy one another." (*Second Essay Concerning Civil Government, Great Books of the Western World*, vol. 35).

Notice what Locke is saying here:

1. Those of us in Nature have been given a set of Laws which govern our behavior
2. We are all equal and independent under that law
3. We are all created by the same all-powerful Creator
4. We are the servants of the Creator
5. We are here by the order of the Creator
6. We are here to do the Creator's business

7. We are the property of the Creator
8. As such, we are not free to harm each other by the exercise of our own personal freedoms

To get to the details of the rights that are inherit within this structure of Natural Law, we look to William Blackstone, who wrote:

"Those rights, then, which God and nature have established, and are therefore called natural rights, such as are life and liberty, need not the aid of human laws to be more effectually invested in every man than they are; neither do they receive any additional strength when declared by the municipal laws to be inviolable. On the contrary, no human legislature has power to abridge or destroy them, unless the owner shall himself commit some act that amounts to a forfeiture."

This is what is meant by our founders when they say "unalienable" rights: they are given to us directly by our Creator and are therefore to be respected, protected, and never tread upon by humans or human governments. They are "natural" rights.
Then, barely a decade before the Declaration of Independence was written, Blackstone penned the following:

"And these natural rights may be reduced to three principal or primary articles: the right of personal security, the right of personal liberty; and the right of private property; because as there is no other known method of compulsion, or of abridging man's natural free will, but by an infringement or diminution of one or other of these important rights, the preservation of these, inviolate, may justly be said to include the preservation of our civil immunities in their largest and most extensive sense."

So Blackstone summarizes man's natural rights into three main categories:

1. Personal security
2. Private property
3. Personal liberty

Any time a government, individual, or body of any kind infringes upon these three basic, God-given rights, according to Blackstone, a violation of God's laws is occurring. It certainly makes one wonder about the current state of affairs in our countries today, where the government, the court system, and other powers that be are allowed, under the law, to infringe on each of these.

One can see a clear progression of thought here. Going from Cicero's declaration that there is a Natural Law provided by a Natural Law Giver, and Locke's testament that we have rights that are inherent under that Law, and Blackstone delineation of what those specific rights are, we can see the philosophical thread, congruent with a scriptural world view, that took shape to form the basis of America's founding in freedom.

AUSTRIAN ECONOMICS, PETER SCHIFF, & THE BAILOUTS

Economics seems to be the least understood of the sciences. Economics affects every person that desires to provide for his family, but most people rely on government or the media for their (usually incorrect) snippets on economics. The so-called Austrian School of economics (it is really just actual, historical economics and needs no special name) has the most logical descriptions of what occurs in an economic transaction and aligns with my personal experiences. I believe that to learn economics properly, you must read and then apply the principles to your own endeavors.

We have watched the U.S. government since the 1920's take over our economic freedoms. With every loss of economic freedoms, political and religious freedoms are sure to be lost also. Ludwig von Mises is my favorite author in economics, but may be a little deep for one's first economics exposure. Paul Pilzer's *Unlimited Wealth*, Warren Brookes' *Economy in Mind*, and Friedrich Von Hayek's classic, *The Road to Serfdom*, will give a great foundation for understanding what is happening in the economy today. Ludwig Von Mises' magnum opus, *Human Action*, is my favorite book on economics ever written.

If we observe our economy today we will see major violations of economic law. The sad thing is that the government will violate economic law with its interventionist policies and then when those fail, the government blames free enterprise. This allows the government to do *even more* interventionist policies. It is similar to a mad doctor who gives the patient a drug that makes the patient worse. The doctor then states the patient is very sick and will need further drug injections. The process ends only in the death of the patient.

Socialism/Communism has never worked anywhere! I hear all these poetic words on the joy of government regulations and control to stop the greedy entrepreneur, but in Cuba, North Korea, Soviet Union, etc, they only succeeded in stopping their economy. The Austrian school of economics recognizes that all economies rise and fall on the economic calculations and predictions of the entrepreneur. If you kill the entrepreneur then you kill the catalyst for the entire economy. China has transformed itself into a pseudo-free enterprise country by allowing entrepreneurial profits. The Chinese totalitarians saw the economic writing on the wall and modified their economics (in a blatant disregard of their Marxian roots) to maintain power.

Peter D. Schiff is the president of Euro Pacific Capital Inc., a brokerage firm based in Darien, Connecticut. He is a follower of the Austrian school of economics and has predicted our current crisis years in advance. Schiff, by using the logical conclusions drawn from economic analysis, predicted the credit crisis, the housing devaluations, and many more of the economic maladies we are seeing as reality today. There is a video of news programs where Peter was laughed and mocked for his economic views. He stood his ground throughout, however, and never gave in. Like the old saying goes, "A man with the facts is not at the mercy of a man with an opinion." I salute Peter Schiff for his economic stands against the hysteria of the crowds. We need more men and women that learn the truth of economics for themselves so we will not be led down rabbit holes by our government and the media.

So learn economics for yourself. Knowledge is insulation against being misled by media pundits and self-seeking government "officials."

There is only one way in which a person acquires a new idea: by the combination or association of two or more ideas he already has into a new juxtaposition in such a manner as to discover a relationship among them of which he was not previously aware
- Francis A. Cartier

A THESIS

I have been thinking a lot recently about the current challenges to liberty and how it seems a society like ours is bent on destroying itself from the inside out. In words I've used before, the question is, "How did we get here?" In an attempt to answer this question I have posited four reasons:

1. People are too quick to trust their government.
2. People don't notice the creeping infringement upon their freedoms by their government.
3. People don't understand or appreciate their freedom adequately, nor truly realize how it came to be, or how bad things would be without it.
4. Many are more interested in their own personal advantages than in justice for all, resulting in a "justice for us" mindset.

If we could correct these four deficiencies in the mindset of our fellow citizens, we could stand freedom safely back upon its foundations.

It is easy to take liberty for granted, when you have never had it taken from you. - Dick Cheney

We on this continent should never forget that men first crossed the Atlantic not to find soil for their ploughs but to secure liberty for their souls. - Robert J. McCracken

For what avail the plough or sail, or land or life, if freedom fail? - Ralph Waldo Emerson

IGNORANCE DESTROYS BEAUTY

Watching the death of freedom is heartbreaking. The magnificent construct called the United States of America was built by a collection of talent the likes of which the world has rarely seen. For a crowded moment in time, in a small strip of sea-side colonies, some of the greatest minds ever assembled put aside their sundry differences and collaborated to produce an experiment in government that literally changed the world. Whether or not you are an American citizen reading this, it is unarguable that you have been affected by what those men did two-and-a-half centuries ago.

What the United States founding fathers accomplished was something that had never been done before, and although often copied, has never been duplicated. Their Constitution, and the Bill of Rights upon which the ratification of the Constitution hinged, are literally works of art. They satisfy every concept of the term: 1) solving a complex problem 2) doing so elegantly 3) and moving the audience while in the process.

This work of art was chiseled out of the Judeo-Christian world-view, founded upon a strong distrust of government power, polished with the principles of justice *for all*, and finished with the sanctity of the individual and his or her right to *life, liberty,* and the *pursuit of happiness.* This masterpiece was then bestowed upon the people as a guardian of their freedoms against governmental tyranny.

Today, however, the administration in Washington and its Congress are defacing this work of art as though it were just another dusty heirloom. I heard one analogy that it's as if the teenagers have taken over the principle's office; weilding the power without any understanding of how it got there or what it is for. For some reason, in a cruder illustration, my mind goes back to the old Kevin Costner movie *Dances with Wolves*, in which a disenfranchised Civil War veteran finds himself in love with an Indian woman. Throughout the middle of the movie Costner's character writes a beautiful and moving diary of his feelings and experiences but loses it as he is re-captured by his countrymen. In a display of arrogance and insolence, one of the soldiers, unable to read, used the diary as toilet paper.

Every time I think of that analogy it strikes me as somewhat offensive, and perhaps it is a bit too strong for use here. But I use it to demonstrate a simple truth: ignorance destroys beauty. What is happening in Washington right now can only be described as ignorance. If it is not ignorance, then it must be something much worse, for who would knowingly and in full understanding trample something so beautiful?

There are many fronts on which we could discuss the new and proposed policies coming out of Washington:

1. Moral grounds (as in, It's not *Right!*)
2. Equitable Grounds (as in, it's not *Fair!*)
3. Constitutional Grounds (as in, it's not *Authorized!)*

These would all warrant complete articles of their own. These three, however, are easily opposed by people with strange worldviews. Without a Judeo-Christian ethos, moral grounds become relative, and without absolutes, who's to say what is moral? For someone playing the victim card, the second one disappears as such a person only wants *justice for them* and not *justice for all*. For power-lovers the Constitution can easily be trampled in the name of expediency. So, arguments for these three reasons often fall upon deaf ears.

The fourth front, however, is unarguable, or should be. It is supported by history, facts, and adequate experimentation around the world. The fourth category is:

4. Pragmatics (as in, it's not *workable!*)

Even if we leave off speaking about moral absolutes, fairness and justice, and the constructs of law through the Constitution and Bill of Rights, we are still left with the extremely important understanding of *what works*. And quite simply the policies being passed into law in Washignton right now do not work. Outrageous government spending (which, by the way, happened to catastrophic levels under George W. Bush's adminstration, as well), does not stimulate the economy, but wrecks it. Abortion does not help a society, it destroys it. Befriending terrorists does not appease them, it emboldens them. Celebrating diversity does not unite, it divides.* Nationalizing private industry does not lead to productivty gains, but to the death of competitiveness. Nationalizing health care does not lead to better care for all, but to worse care for most. Eliminating guns does not lead to less gun crime, just less protection *against* gun crimes.

I could go further, but my point should be clear. These things are not theories left untried, but are a compilation of failed policies from other nations and history that have *crashed miserably every time they've been tried*! As I have said before why must we repeat bad policy just to make sure it's still bad?

Ignorance, my friends.

Or worse.

---

*Placing emphasis on diversity over unity is not the proper answer to the racial and other injustices of the past. We do not become stronger by seperating into groups of "us vs. them." This is not to say, of course, that we deny our individual and distinct heritages. It merely states the principle that too much emphasis on our differences and not enough on our commonalities is disunifying. By constantly calling people "Caucasion" or "Latino" or "African" Americans, instead of just "Americans," we are not really speaking to what the concept of collective freedom is all about. The reason the Constitution was and is so powerful is that it stood as a mighty reminder to the hypocrisy of a country that hadn't yet lived up to its words. This eventually brought an end to slavery and birthed the Civil Rights movement. But overcompensation and incorrect emphasis deny the document its cohesive power to unite and instead give way to disintegration. We have been sold the concept of diversity as a virtue so much that it often goes unquestioned. I myself prefer unity, the unity of a people under a founding document of freedom and justice FOR ALL.

MOMENTS OF GREATNESS

Way back when I was a teenaged motocross junkie one of my heroes was Ricky Johnson, a multiple Outdoor National and Supercross Champion. On several occasions I got to see him race in person, and each time it was a treat. I have always admired greatness, and seeing Ricky Johnson at the prime of his motorcycle career was an inspiration.

Today, Mr. Johnson is one of the country's top dirt truck racers. In a movie documenting the incredible Baja 1000 desert race, Ricky Johnson was interviewed. I found his comments very prescient, and one of the best descriptions of "living in the zone" that I have ever heard. Here is what he said:

"I've had what I consider a few moments where I felt greatness, when I raced. A lot of people, if you ask them, will say, break it down, what was your best race? And it might not be they won, but they had a moment. You're so present, and everything is happening effortlessly, flawlessly, while outside it's utter chaos, it's chaos all around 'em. And they're sitting in the middle of the tornado, the eye of the storm. You make a correction before a reaction starts. They're not scared, they're not afraid, and they don't think they can get hurt. You don't have time to be afraid. Afraid comes afterwards! It's not because you're crazy or you've got a death wish. It's competition. Fighters don't' fight to hurt people, they fight to win. Races don't race because they want to die, they want to go fast, and that's my high. That's the way I manipulate my life, is through the mechanics of a machine."

A big part of successful living is doing what you do to the fullest extent of your abilities. Somewhere in that range lies "the zone;" the place where all the fulfillment of God's promise in you comes into broad relief. You are doing what you were built to do and in harmony with all that you've ever wanted to become.

As Ricky Johnson described it, he manipulates race machinery to forge a life that keeps him in the zone, to keep himself alive and pushing to become great at what he was created to do. Each of us has that kind of greatness deep inside. We were built to accomplish and push and strive to utilize all the gifts God has given us. Each of us was given our own arena in which to compete. It may not be off-road racing (which is a shame), but there is a special calling within each person waiting to be fulfilled. It's inside of that calling that one feels what Mr. Johnson labors to explain in this fascinating quote.

So do what you do, while you can. There will be a day when your chance has passed, when your "racing" days are done. What would you give, in that time, to go back and have one more lap? One more mile? One more opportunity to live "in the zone?"

The key to a life that counts is seeing these truths in advance, realizing that there are doors that won't stay open forever, and knowing you've got to charge through them while you can!

Attitude is a little thing that makes a big difference"
- Winston Churchill

Every day may not be good, but there's something good in every day. - Author Unknown

I have never met a man so ignorant that I couldn't learn something from him. - Galileo Galilei

The man who has no inner life is a slave to his surroundings.
- Henri Frédéric Amiel

GIVE VALIDATION

The longer I live, the more I realize the essential hunger inside of everyone to be accepted, approved and appreciated. If we, as human beings, could all learn to focus on others before focusing on ourselves, we would overcome so many of the problems that plague our society today. If we desire acceptance in life, then we must *give* acceptance. If we desire approval in life, then we must *give* approval. If we desire appreciation in life, then we must *give* appreciation. If we desire validation in life then we must *give* validation, and if we desire smiles then we must *give* a smile.

I know people can accuse me, a former engineer, of losing my rationality and falling into sentimentality, but I know what I speak is true. A sincerely thought-out and spoken or written comment can fuel a person for a week. I know many high achievers and it is as true for them as it is for a young child. As it is said, Recognition: grown men die for it and babies cry for it. Do not hoard this precious gift. Do not feel that complimenting and praising others takes from you. Appreciation is one of the few gifts that the more you give it away, the more it returns to you. You will gather more bees with honey than vinegar. There is a shortage of honey and stockpiles of vinegar in life.

I want to thank all of my friends and family for many kind words and encouraging statements. I will never be able to share how much they have meant to me. The world tends to beat the joy out of you, but you still have the choice of whether to surrender it. If you have ever lost your joy, then choose now to reclaim it by giving away joy to others. Start a virtuous cycle of sincere praise and appreciation and change the world one life at a time!

BECOME A CULTIVATOR

Days pass into weeks, weeks into months, months to years, and, well, you know how it goes. In fact, the older you are the more you are familiar with the frenzied acceleration of age.

"Leaders understand their natural network of friends and acquaintances is one of their biggest treasures."

The thing to consider, though, as these moments race by in a blur, is the lives of others around you. Leaders understand their natural network of friends and acquaintances is one of their biggest treasures. Not only does this web of connectedness provide business contacts and leads, but more importantly, the very spice of life. After all, we are here to serve others!

There are three approaches people take toward their hubs-of-connectedness (or networks):

1. Passivity
2. Destruction
3. Cultivation

I believe each of these categories is obvious. We all know people who take little notice of others in their life, or on the contrary, who destroy relationships and contacts with habitually combative behavior. The most productive, fulfilled people, however, are those who actively pursue relationships and friendships.

There are many constructive steps toward becoming a cultivator. Caring and being interested in other people are prerequisites. Communicating regularly is a must. Listening to and knowing the other person is important. What is the other person's dominant personality type? What is their Love Language? What motivates them? What scares them? Being dependable, reliable, and loyal builds trust over the long haul. Honesty and fairness generate a momentum of their own, over time. And don't forget the power of providing encouragement and support.

If you tried you could, no doubt, create a list of your own. In fact, it seems the steps necessary to establishing friendships and relationships are known, in some degree, to us all. Building up a network of quality connections and relationships appears to be nothing more than a choice, for those who are willing to take the effort.

I encourage you to take some of those steps today. Call someone. Send a text. Write a note. Catch someone in the act of doing something right. Let someone know you care. Believe me, the world needs it! And once you see the boomerang-effect of cultivating relationships, you'll realize you need it too.

Leaders who win the respect of others are the ones who deliver more than they promise, not the ones who promise more than they can deliver. - Mark A. Clement

Napoleon was asked after his stunning victory in Italy how he made his army cross the Alps. He replied, "One does not make a French army cross the Alps; one leads it across."

JAMES "BUSTER" DOUGLAS VS. MIKE TYSON - A REAL LIFE DAVID VS. GOLIATH

I have always pulled for the underdogs vs. the over-confident champs. America loves a great upset and its history has provided many examples of them. One of my all-time favorite sports moments was the "Buster" Douglas vs. Mike Tyson fight. No one gave Douglas a chance, but he had dedicated the fight to his recently deceased mother. When a person knows "why" he is doing something he can endure almost any "how".

There are moments in every person's life when they must defeat their Goliaths. We need more David's in leadership who will stand for truth and conviction instead of ease and comfort. Here are some special takes from this great moment in sports history.

1. Mike Tyson's opponent, as usual, was paid little heed. Champions are knocked-out when they stop respecting the competitors and develop a deity complex: thinking they are infallible and can do no wrong.
2. Opponents were terrified of Mike Tyson. Opponents should let the champion read the press clippings. The opponent should be focused on strategy to beat the over-confident champ.
3. "Buster" Douglas was another heavyweight that looked like a "sitting duck". It is not important what the crowd says, but what you feel and think inside your own mind that matters most.
4. Douglas was for this one big occasion going to be the fighter of his dreams! When a person knows why they do what they do and focuses on the end goal, great things can happen.
5. Fear was a major part of Tyson's weaponry. Tyson relied on the

fear of his opponent to mentally defeat him.

6. The fighters came in frozen like the prey of a cobra. It was quickly obvious that "Buster" Douglas did not fear Mike Tyson.

7. "Buster" Douglas's mother had just died and he felt he had nothing to lose by giving his all in memory of her.

8. Tyson had begun to go on emotional rampages. This occurs with people and companies who develop a deity complex.

9. Tyson refused to run and develop his lung capacity. Champions who fall no longer feel they need to do the disciplined work.

10. Tyson's manager said to him, "You are not Superman, and the things you are doing, you are heading for a butt whuppin."

11. The announcers thought "Buster" was going to his doom, but "Buster" knew better!

12. Incredibly, the self proclaimed "Baddest Man on the Planet" (Tyson) was struggling in the ring.

And David defeated Goliath!

OUR AMERICAN HERITAGE -
EDUCATING THE ELECTORATE IS THE KEY

"A nation of well informed men who have been taught to know and prize the rights which God has given them cannot be enslaved. It is in the region of ignorance that tyranny begins."
- Benjamin Franklin

It is time to consider the lowering standards for spiritual, political, economic, and historical literacy in America. I fear for our country when people can be whipped into a mass frenzy by a speaker's style more than his substance. Now don't misread me here. I believe strongly in having a pleasing public speaking style, but that should be secondary to the truth of the speaker's statements. To follow someone because of their communication skills with no understanding of the underlying message is a breeding ground for disaster.

Without an understanding of our American heritage, how are American voters discerning between the spiritual, economic, political and historical issues? Without a basic understanding of our American history all decisions are chosen upon how they make people feel, not on what people think. Sadly, in today's society, belligerent ignorance is as highly valued as diligent study. You can look at any comment sections of any public blog to see the truth of this statement.

"Whenever the people are well-informed, they can be trusted with their own government." - Thomas Jefferson

Thinking requires a general knowledge of the subject at hand.

I cannot have an educated discussion on Albanian politics, because I do not have all of the issues and their historical relevance at my fingertips. If I were asked to be involved in a discussion on the subject, I would have to do some homework to get up to speed. Every four years, people place a vote for the most powerful person in the world. I have wondered, for years, how much homework they have done to prepare for this nearly sacred honor. I am not one of the people who believes that image is everything. In fact, I am one of the people who believes the exact opposite. Give me character over reputation any day of the week. I have learned enough about the media to understand their goal is to paint an image. But as John Wooden says, "Reputation is what people say you are and character is who you are." Just like a book, I focus on the content of the book, not just its cover. If I had to choose, I would take great content with a poor cover than the reverse. In order to understand the content, you must be educated on the principles yourself.

> *"Reputation is what people say you are and character is who you are."*
> -John Wooden

"Liberty cannot be preserved without general knowledge among the people." - John Adams

"I know of no safe repository of the ultimate power of society but people. And if we think them not enlightened enough, the remedy is not to take the power from them, but to inform them by education." - Thomas Jefferson

"If a nation expects to be ignorant and free, it expects what never was and never can be." - Thomas Jefferson

Our founders gave us a nearly perfect form of government, that combined responsibility and accountability. It gave us the responsibility to hold our government accountable for its actions. However, in our prosperity, we have been lulled to sleep. Sadly, most of us think the type of government we have is a democracy. The better educated can proudly say that we have a republic. However, among those better educated, not one in a thousand understands the true substantive difference between the two.

There are two main reasons for the dilemma in which we find ourselves:

1. We are prosperous—the most prosperous nation on earth, and our prosperity has made us comfortable, and in our comfort, we have abrogated our duties to those who promise to do them for us without any serious scrutiny. And as generations pass we grow more firm in our lack of understanding, and we do not even know the standards to which our officials should be held.
2. The deliberate "dumbing down" of our education system in an effort to enslave the public through ignorance and prepare them for world government.

"We have no government armed with power capable of contending with human passions unbridled by morality and religion. Avarice, ambition, revenge, or gallantry, would break the strongest cords of our Constitution as a whale goes through a net. Our Constitution was made only for a moral and religious people. It is wholly inadequate to the government of any other." - John Adams

UNSOUND MONEY SYSTEM NEEDED BY GOVERNMENT FOR WEALTH CONFISCATION

Way back before Alan Greenspan became Chairman of the Federal Reserve, he penned a now famous essay for inclusion in Ayn Rand's book, *Capitalism: The Unknown Ideal*. In the article Greenspan explains the stability and logic behind a gold-standard-based money system, and then makes the following observation:

"But the opposition to the gold standard in any form -- from a growing number of welfare-state advocates -- was prompted by a much subtler insight: the realization that the gold standard is incompatible with chronic deficit spending (the hallmark of the welfare state). Stripped of its academic jargon, the welfare state is nothing more than a mechanism by which governments confiscate the wealth of the productive members of a society to support a wide variety of welfare schemes."

Two major points can be seen in this small excerpt:

1. Our government does not want a sound money system because it would not allow them to get away with deficit spending
2. Inflation and deficit spending are a hidden way the government can take from the productive and give to the free-loaders

Our nation is in an ideological war between those who want to ride in the cart and those who are pulling it. For too long the cart-pullers have allowed themselves to become loaded down with sneaky, subtle, guilt-inflicting, victim-mentality, falsely-compassionate, welfare-state-minded free-loaders. Ayn Rand, never one to pull a punch, called these free-loaders "looters."

The original rebellion in the American colonies was instigated by less than 2% taxation! Assuming anyone reading this is a cart-puller and not a free-loader, your likely level of taxation is somewhere between 48 and 64%, after considering federal income tax, property tax, Social Security, Medicare, school and local taxes, sales taxes, gasoline taxes, telephone taxes, tolls, licenses and fees, and in many cases state income tax.

According to author and political commentator Amity Schlaes, fully 40% of the U.S. population is now riding in the cart.

This can not go on much longer.

An idea is a feat of association - Robert Frost

There is one thing stronger than all the armies in the world: and that is an idea whose time has come - Victor Hugo

It's just as sure a recipe for failure to have the right idea fifty years too soon as five years too late - J. R. Platt

DEMOCRACY
IN THE NBA

Warning: This is humor and is meant to be funny and teach some lessons before it's too late! This is not slanted toward either Democrats or Republicans as I feel they have both let the American people down and have lost touch with free enterprise American Ideals!

We would never do in sports what we do as a matter of course in business. Have you ever noticed how business people are portrayed in Hollywood? There is little recognition of their commitment, little celebration of their success, just criticisms for daring to win in a free enterprise business. Free enterprise is designed to separate the wheat from the chaff. If you are not good enough you will fail; until you either get good enough or go into another field better suited for your gifts. No stimulus package will change that! This is a non-negotiable economic law. In the following satire I hope you will enjoy learning that we do not help industry by artificially keeping people in the game who have not earned the favor of the customers!

Democracy has spoken. Sources in our all-powerful government have leaked to the press that HOPE NBA is rolling out. HOPE – Helplessly Out-skilled People Entering – NBA is an important government policy designed to give the less fortunate an opportunity to participate and share every boy's dream of playing in the National Basketball Association. For years selfish, greedy athletes with skills given to them through little effort of their own have taken most of the headlines and playing time in the NBA. Our government and many American voters became concerned about this blatant inequality. What about all the overweight, out of shape weekend warrior guys like Fred Snodgrass? Fred has never been given his fair playing chance to show the NBA what he can do. Fred played basketball in the 8th grade and he even collected NBA cards before Magic Johnson and Larry Bird made the NBA cool again.

It is guys like Fred who bought Cleveland season tickets year after year to support these prima donna athletes. Why can't people cheer for Fred once in a while? Is that so hard America? Fred is a lifelong fan and felt something should be done! Fred and his HOPE-NBA political action committee, CRYBABIES – (Committee to Restore Your Belief in American Basketball's Integrity and Equality of Scores) are backed by millions of angry fans and weekend warriors who have vowed to fight until this injustice is corrected. Anyone who can vote can now play in the NBA!

Fred and millions of CRYBABIES utilized the democratic process to vote in a government to bring HOPE and CHANGE – (Collective Handouts Allowing No Grounds for Excellence) in the NBA. Fred believed that he could gather enough votes from other CRYBABIES to bring this type of CHANGE and HOPE to the NBA. Fred envisioned a time sharing plan for the NBA. This would allow the men down on their luck to experience the joy of playing in the new HOPE-NBA. The fact that the NBA players voted against this "fair play stimulus package" just proves their selfish hearts and the denial of the equality principle that America stands for today! Fred pointed to the current NBA players' 100% vote against the stimulus package as further confirmation of government's need to get involved.

Sources say government bureaucrats are working hard to enforce maximum playing times for the selfish All Pros. This will allow the less gifted and committed the time sharing formula necessary to enjoy the American dream. Pictures of Fred Snodgrass practicing with the Cleveland Cavaliers are making the rounds. Imagine what a fairer world it will be when our American government finally limits Lebron James to a maximum of 25 minutes per game and no more than 12 points per game. Why does any NBA player need to score more than 12 points? When is enough, enough? Our government must teach these selfish prima donnas a lesson in fair play. Any points in excess by the All Pros will be pooled and dispersed in a "redistribution stimulus package" to Fred Snodgrass and the other less fortunate wannabe athletes. Imagine the dignity and self respect Fred Snodgrass will feel when he looks at the statistics and he is averaging 12 points per game just like Lebron James! This is an America worth fighting for – results without sacrifice!

CRYBABIES around the country are elated by the latest developments, but many coaches questioned the wisdom of giving weekend warriors so much playing time. One anonymous coach said, "We are faced with international competition that is putting the best of the best on the court night after night. How can we possibly compete when we have CRYBABIES on the court who haven't played the game at this level?" Government officials replied, "Winning games while American CRYBABIES who are just down on their luck sit in the stands is not American anymore. We have to stop the hurting for everyone, even if it means losing games to other nations to ensure equality in America." A gleeful Fred Snodgrass was quoted as saying, "For the first time in my life, I feel proud to be an American. I am an NBA player regardless of my lack of basketball gifts and talents. America is now a place where anyone without talent, training, effort, commitment, or size can play in the NBA. All I did was dwell on my hurts and gather up enough other CRYBABIES who are sick of competing against those selfish winners. We utilized the democratic process with our voting and our government did the rest! I am so proud to be an American!"

Season ticket holders for the Cleveland Cavalier have dropped 25%, but the government is proposing a tax on all citizens to make up the difference in lost revenue. If the tax does not generate enough income to pay the CRYBABIES' salaries, the government will quickly print new money. In the first scrimmage against the Albanian national team, the Americans suffered their first loss ever against this small mountainous country. Fred scored his 12 points, thanks to the stimulus package collected from the excessive points of the All Pros. Lebron James was not available for comment, but sources say that negotiations between the Irish national team and Lebron's agent are underway. Our government, in anticipation of the greedy athletes, has proposed the building of a wall around the entire United States. This will keep athletes in our country to enjoy the benefits of the new HOPE and CHANGE in the NBA. Our government was concerned that without this wall, only CRYBABIES would want to stay in the country to play American basketball.

The Detroit Lions have taken the lead in promoting the same type of HOPE and CHANGE for the NFL. A Detroit Lions official shared his thoughts, "We are sick and tired of attempting to compete against the Pittsburgh Steelers (a greedy group of sports athletes and capitalists) who act like winning trophies is more important than sharing the laurels. The Lions have never won a Super Bowl while the Steelers have six! How is that fair? Many of the less fortunate teams are forming groups to right this obvious wrong. I want to thank our government for having the courage to lead the way in legitimizing this righteous maneuver. In the American past, this was called loser's envy, but today this is equality! Thanks to our government, the Detroit Lions franchise and our fans will no longer be ashamed to be part of the NFL and wear a Lion's jersey."

The American Government is meeting with Major League baseball, the NHL, Tiger Woods and Michael Phelps later this month to review joint plans for HOPE and CHANGE. Welcome to the new fairer, non-competitive America.

Those who expect to reap the blessings of freedom, must, like men, undergo the fatigue of supporting it. - Thomas Paine

In the truest sense, freedom cannot be bestowed; it must be achieved. - Franklin D.Roosevelt

Freedom is the oxygen of the soul. - Moshe Dayan

There are two freedoms - the false, where a man is free to do what he likes; the true, where he is free to do what he ought.
- Charles Kingsley

"ON CALL" AND THE TECHNOLOGY ADDICTION

Just because we *can* do something doesn't mean we *should*. Just because a technology is developed doesn't mean it will improve our lives. Just because something makes communication more convenient doesn't mean it makes it better. Just because we can be contacted anytime, anywhere, for any reason, doesn't mean we should be. And, just because everybody else is doing it doesn't mean it's right.

Years ago a practice was developed among doctors where partners would take turns scheduling time to be "on call." This was a way of splitting coverage for the time when all of them would be away from the office but still have the requirement of providing urgent care and answers for their collective group of patients. This was originally looked upon as a special responsibility of the medical profession since medical situations could not be made to conform to office hours. It was and is still an effective practice. Participating doctors agree not to leave the geographic area and vow to remain accessible. This has always been considered a significant commitment and part of what justified the high compensation medical professionals received. Such a burdensome program was rotated among the partners in order to share the load.

Then came thousands of inventions designed to "improve our lives." In just over fifteen years, cell phones went from being carried in large bags and used for emergencies to being attached to every adult, teen, and adolescent like binkies in a nursery. Now, without realizing it, *everybody* has voluntarily placed themselves "on call." Only they haven't done it for a weekend here and another there, they've done it for every day of their lives! Statistics show that an amazing 61% of Americans check e-mail every day while on vacation! And by the way, only 14% of Americans ever take two weeks of vacation at a time to begin with!

We've got e-mail and its annoying notifications, instant messages providing constant interruption, text messages and voice mails. We are awash in means and methods of communication that increase the talk and decrease the listening. After a while one becomes numb.

Remember the famous Thoreau statement: "Most men lead lives of quiet desperation." The only thing that has changed from Thoreau's time is the quiet. It's gone. Today, men lead lives of desperation amongst an endless stream of noise, interruption, and dwindling opportunities for the important moments in life; moments without a chime or a beep or a ring. Moments without an electronic addiction of any kind. Moments of freedom.

My father never once got interrupted by a cell phone call when he played football catch with me in the backyard. He certainly never threw the ball while pinching a phone to his ear with his elbow (as I see at least seventy-five percent of the time in parks and yards. Look for yourself). I never once heard my mom say to me in the car, "Quiet! I'm on the phone!" When my parents were with me, they were *with* me. This is true today only in extreme cases of either chance, or with parents wise enough to fight back.

It makes me wonder. Before we got hit with this onslaught of technological "improvements," did we ever stop to ask whether they would make things better? Of course not. Nobody could have seen how frenzied things would become in just fifteen years, nor how addicted people would be to their needless interruptions and electronic tethers. Besides, we are a society that always assumes more is better, that technology is always an improvement, and that the relentless push forward can always be called progress.

I disagree. We have given up something precious; and we have barely noticed.

"Happiness is an attitude. We either make ourselves miserable, or happy and strong. The amount of work is the same."
- Francesca Reigler

BLIND SPOTS

There is a saying that I have always liked: "The difference between self-perception and reality is often enormous."

The size of that difference is called a "blind spot." Unfortunately, we all have them. Perhaps the way you chew your food drives people crazy. Or maybe you interrupt others constantly and annoy them as a result. But these examples are really just foibles; small little mannerisms that we all have that don't really reflect our character. While it might be helpful for us to identify these blind spots in our mannerisms, these things are not "majors" in and of themselves.

> *"The difference between self-perception and reality is often enormous."*

What *are* majors are blind spots of character and relationships. I see people who live in a world full of blind spots about themselves, and these blind spots cause pain and friction.

Why is it so hard to identify these things in ourselves? I am not sure, but if they were easier to spot, we'd probably call them "fuzzy spots" or something. But blind spots are blind spots because they are truly unobservable to us.

Unless we take the time to look. Unless we have an open mind to mentorship. Unless we will take responsibility, not only for our own actions, but for the results that surround us in our lives. By looking at such evidence, we are installing a "blind spot mirror" on our life. Here is what I mean: Let's say that in most places in your life there is conflict. You have troubles with your mother. You have an ongoing feud with your brother. You have had a major fight with your spouse in the past thirty days. You have people who were previously friends who don't talk to you now. You have left churches and jobs in the past year or two because of conflict with others. Your children are rebels. Your neighbor is a jerk. Your in-laws are idiots. Your business partners and teammates are driving you crazy. If you look at results such as these, there is only one conclusion you can make: these people are all to blame! I know you are laughing because no one in their right might could ever come to such a conclusion. It should be obvious that the problem in this scenario is the person at the center of it all! That is why we call it a blind-spot.

There are people (swarms of them, bless their hearts) who are like this and see absolutely nothing wrong with themselves. I often picture their funeral, when people gather around and whisper nice things, but think back to the pain and the hurt and wish it hadn't been that way. If only they'd have realized how damaging they were to people. If only they'd realized how abrasive and destructive they were. If only they would have taken responsibility for their results and the impact they were having on the people around them. If only they would have been open to feedback, to mentoring, to input, to the abstract possibility that they were to blame for the poor results in their life! If only, if only, if only . . . .

This is just one example, and a tragic one, at that. But there are others. Let's say the evidence suggests a lack of purpose or drive or ambition or hunger or whatever you want to call it. You didn't get good grades at school, but that was because the teachers were uninspiring. You didn't do well at your first job, but that was because you were discriminated against for being young. You didn't get that promotion, but that's because you went to the wrong university. You didn't get that exciting new project, but that's because someone else was closer to the boss. You didn't hit that business goal, but that's because your spouse made other demands on you. You didn't attend that big event, but that's because you had other plans. You didn't, you didn't, you didn't. See the pattern in this one? Is it really the "fault" of all those outside factors, or would the person at the center of this be the cause?

When we lay it out all logically and clinically like this it is so clear. Everybody comes to the same conclusion and shakes their heads at the poor people with blind spots, glad that it is not them. But what I'm here to tell you is that we all have blind spots. And it is highly possible that our biggest blind spot is thinking that we don't have one to begin with!

And by the way, our blind spots are usually only invisible to us. *Everybody* else sees them clearly.

So what is your blind spot? What does the evidence tell you? Take this question seriously, and do something about it. Trust me, people are praying that you will figure it out!

A good leader takes a little more than his share of blame, a little less than his share of credit." - Arnold Glasgow

In calm water every ship has a good captain.
- Swedish proverb

LEADERS BUILD RELATIONSHIPS

One of the key components in a leader's effectiveness is his or her ability to build and foster positive, strong, and productive relationships. Often, this part of the "art" of leadership is overlooked. Some seem to think that leadership means authority, position, or power. Rather, leadership is the influence of other people through a strong vision, through the example and character of the leader, and ultimately through the quality of the relationships that are built and the quality of the individuals with whom those relationships are built.

Finding good people and forging tight relationships with them are not an option for a leader.

Finding good people and forging tight relationships with them are not an option for a leader. Once these relationships are established, a leader then must be capable of maintaining them. Some people are great at first impressions and quick friendships. Others are better the more people get to know them. Great leaders are both. And don't underestimate this: it takes different skills to start relationships than it does to maintain and strengthen them over time.

Strong relationships make for strong organizations. When the winds of adversity blow, it is the bond of strong relationships that holds things together. Influence, changing things for the better, and attaining a vision are all brought about through powerful relationships.

What are you doing on a daily basis to improve your ability to build relationships? Have you established the connections you need with the kind of people you require to achieve your dreams and visions? Remember: all accomplishment is with, through, and for people. None of us are an island. We must accomplish all things by dealing with people. Even "individual" activities like painting and golf are worthless without customers, patrons, fans, competitors, and admirers. Yes, like it or not, God put us here to serve Him and to serve others. That's what leaders do. So get "other-minded," find people to forge tight, sincere, lasting relationships with, and set about together to achieve great things. It's the only way it ever happens!

CHURCHILL OVERCOMES

Winston Churchill is practically a leadership cliché. His defiance in the face of Nazi aggression during World War II is deservingly legendary. But the back story behind Sir Winston's rise (and fall, and rise again) is quite incredible. His story is one of determination, deliberate personal growth, perseverance, courage, and vision.

Young Winston Churchill was not a good student, and in his younger years was ranked toward the bottom of his class. As a boy, he talked with a lisp and also stuttered. To fix this, he practiced for hours in front of a mirror until his pronunciations were correct. Most people don't realize, as well, that Churchill was held as a prisoner of war during the Boer War in South Africa. From this predicament, let's begin a timeline of accomplishments and defeats in the life of this incredible leader (from Jeff O'Leary, *Footprints in Time*):

1899 - While serving as army lieutenant, he is captured, escapes, and temporarily rejoins the army

1900 - Elected to Parliament, Conservative Party

1908 - Marries Clementine Hozier

1911-1915 - Serves as First Lord of the Admiralty (similar to Secretary of the Navy in the U.S.)

1915 - Held responsible for the Dardanelles disaster at Gallipoli -

250,000 Allied casualties. Forced to resign, offered a cabinet post without influence. At age 40, rejoins the army in France and leads a battalion. All media and both parties declare Churchill finished.

1917 - Writes proposal on building a tank with caterpillar tracks. Tank called "Churchill's Folly" until it proves itself in battle and results in his appointment as minister of munitions.

1919 - Appointed to secretary of state for War and Air.

1921 - Rises to cabinet post of Colonial Secretary (similar to Secretary of State in U.S., overseeing Colonial Empire).

1923 - Runs again for Parliament as a Liberal. Loses.

1924 - Runs as an Independent. Loses.

1924-1929 - Appointed chancellor of the Exchequer (second to the Prime Minister)

1930 - Party out of power following the stock market crash and Depression. Churchill retains seat in Parliament. Loses nearly all his wealth in the Great Depression and begins writing.

1930-1939 - Loses all influence in both parties as he advocates for a stronger military. A vocal opponent of Neville Chamberlain's appeasement policy with Germany, his warnings fall on deaf ears. Publishes four books during the decade, but the prevailing wisdom declares he is finished.

1939 - Chamberlain returns from Germany, waving treaty document and proclaiming, "Peace in our time." Churchill responds, "You were given the choice between war and dishonor. You have chosen both!"

1939 - Hitler breaks pact with Chamberlain and invades Poland

May 1940 - Chamberlain forced to resign as Prime Minister.

Summer 1940 - Churchill appointed to first term as Prime Minister.

In 1939 the German Army had 98 divisions available for the invasion of Poland. Although some were ill-equipped veteran reservists, they still had 1.5 million well-trained men available for action. It also had 9 panzer divisions. Each one had 328 tanks . . . When the German Army mounted its Western Offensive in 1940, it had had 2.5 million men and 2500 tanks . . . The German Army continued to grow and in June 1941 had 3 million men (including 200,000 from its allies) . . . available for Operation Barbarossa against the Soviet Union. This included 142 infantry divisions, 17 panzer divisions and 4,000 tanks . . . Despite heavy losses in the Soviet Union and in France following the D-Day landings, the German Army still had 168 infantry divisions and 25 panzer divisions by January 1945.

In January 1942 the United States could field only 37 army divisions, one of which was fully trained, equipped, and battle ready. From the fall of 1939 to the summer of 1940, tens of millions of Europeans lost their freedom to fascism with frightening speed.

Poland was attacked first and fell to Germany in twenty-seven days.

Germany attacked Finland in November 1939 and forced a peace agreement in March 1940.

Germany invaded Norway and Denmark in April 1940 and at the same time, France, Belgium, Luxembourg, and the Netherlands. Belgium surrendered in May, Norway surrendered in June, and France surrendered after less than thirty days of combat, in spite of its ability to mobilize more than 5 million men. Hitler entered Paris on June 23, 1940.

In July 1940, the Soviets seized Lithuania, Latvia, Estonia, and eastern Poland. Italy occupied British territories in East Africa, while the United States continued to remain officially neutral, and Germany launched its attack on the last remaining free nation in Europe - Great Britain. It appeared that Europe and the rest of the world would soon have a German dictator replacing their freely elected governments. Britain was about to face the darkest days of its history - alone.

Great Britain would stand alone, for a while, but it would not be without leadership. Into this void stepped a man who had for years warned of the Nazi threat, and who had spent his entire life overcoming obstacles and preparing himself for his great destiny. Churchill's resolve and determination put a face on courage that rallied a nation to its "finest hour." As Churchill himself said, "It is a crime to despair. We must learn to draw from misfortune the means of future strength."

> *It is a crime to despair. We must learn to draw from misfortune the means of future strength."*
> - Winston Churchill

But there is more to the story. After World War II ended, another power vacuum developed. The fall of Nazism in Europe brought a land and power-hunger Russia into Eastern Europe. Communism was quick to bite off large chunks of territory surrendered by the Nazis. Most of the world was so war-weary and thrilled about the prospect of peace that they were willing to interpret events in Eastern Europe with rose-colored glasses. But not Churchill. He vehemently opposed Communist advances, and he vocally warned of its threat. But the world was ready for peace, and Churchill once again lost power. Not long after standing firm in Britain's finest hour, the master leader fell from power and was again out of the government. Only later did the people realize, once again, that Churchill had been right, and once again made him Prime Minister. But it was too late. The Cold War had begun.

Churchill's life is so full of inspiration that any leader can find a lesson from which to gain strength and wisdom. Time and again Churchill stood for what was right, and it often cost him dearly. He overcame obstacles and opposition throughout his storied career. He met foes head on. He rose from the ashes after every defeat. He made mistakes, learned from them, and lived to redeem himself. Sometimes he had a following, sometimes he didn't.

As O'Leary wrote, "Character is not born - character is formed. Begin with yourself. Perhaps your inclination is to cave in when the pressures grow and the obstacles seem impossible to overcome. You must develop a strategy to reinforce your attitude and spirit at times like these. Perhaps one way is to realize you aren't the first and only person to ever face insurmountable odds." If this is true, then Churchill's example ought to suffice!

DO LEADERS MAKE HISTORY OR DOES HISTORY MAKE LEADERS?

Every great leader knows the feeling of being caught up in the momentum of a great cause. True leaders live for those moments and exert every ounce of their ability to push things along toward their ultimate vision. For a leader, there is perhaps nothing more exhilarating than having one's efforts lead to results that are in line with the highest picture the leader has of his or her self, goal, and vision.

It has been said that trying times reveal a leader's character. Another statement says that "wars make heroes." Certainly there is something to be said for the times themselves being at least a little responsible for presenting opportunities for a leader to thrive. After all, doesn't it make sense that there are hundreds of generals just as capable as the ones who became famous during war time, but never really achieved fame and notoriety because there was no war to make them known?

On the other hand, it also makes sense that a leader can impact those around him and even alter the course of events. Certainly a leader's efforts make a difference. A leader's efforts often have an enormous impact. Who would lead if the efforts of a leader made no difference?

Considering these two points of view reveals a paradox. Namely, that events make leaders, but leaders also make events. To what extent is either one of these positions true? To answer that question, I would like to quote from a distinguished professor at the University of Southern California (in fact, he's USC's President), Steven B. Sample:

"In the course on leadership that Warren Bennis and I teach at USC, we contrast the views of Leo Tolstoy, who believed that history shapes and determines leaders, with those of Thomas Carlyle, who believed that leaders shape and determine history. In his epilogue to perhaps the greatest of all novels, *War and Peace*, Tolstoy argued that kings and generals are history's slaves. That is, Tolstoy believed that leaders merely ride the crests of historical waves which have been set in motion by myriad forces beyond these leaders' control or comprehension. 'Every act of theirs, which appears to them an act of their own free will," he wrote, 'is in an historical sense involuntary and is related to the whole cause of history and predestined from eternity.'

On the other side is Carlyle, the nineteenth-century British historian and essayist, who was convinced that 'history is the biography of great men,' the greatest of them being kings. The very word king, Carlyle contends, derives from the ancient word can-ning, which means 'alble man.' In Carlyle's view, it is the Ablemen (and Ablewomen) of our species who direct the course of history and determine humanity's destiny.

My experiences as a leader, as well as my study of chaos theory and related phenomena, have led me to a middle ground between Tolstoy and Carlyle. It may well be that our world is largely Tolstoyan, subject to historical forces which no man or woman can fully measure and analyze, and the consequences of which no person can fully predict. Thus, to that extent, leaders are in fact history's slaves. However, I am also convinced that Ablemen and Ablewomen can make a difference in the course of human events; that the decisions of leaders can indeed have a lasting impact on the world; that historical determinism is never totally in control."

Several reflections are warranted here, I think. First, I believe that the truth lies between what Tolstoy represents and what Carlyle proclaims. Secondly, I also believe that we cannot properly have this discussion without considering the fact that our world is governed by its Creator, who somehow all-knowingly directs events to His glory, even while at the same time allowing us free will (another of life's greatest paradoxes). Thirdly, and closely related to the second, I believe that we each have a destiny that God has laid upon our hearts to discover, that when pursued, will undoubtedly make a difference. And fourthly, I believe that the most important thing a leader can do is to seek to make an impact in the lives of other people, to a greater extent than he or she works to influence events. In this way, much of the discussion of how much events affect the leader, or visa versa, recedes into the background; for there can be no doubting the fact that one person can and does make a huge impact in the lives of others. Caring for someone, showing them love, forgiving them, considering their needs, serving them, and the whole host of Biblical requirements falling under the category of "love thy neighbor" are all traits of great leaders, and are all certainly effective in the lives of others. In essence, we may compel events, and sometimes events will compel us, but we can always make a difference in the lives of others.

GOVERNMENT SPENDING, KEYNESIAN ECONOMICS, AND POLITICAL RESPONSIBILITY

Since World War II, Keynesian economics has been the main current in economic thought in America. I have taught that "Ideas have Consequences" for years and we are now reaping the bitter harvest of this poor set of ideas. Anyone that would take a cursory look at the economic indicators and our government's budget would have to admit something has gone drastically wrong since World War II. Deficit spending has skyrocketed, savings for Americans are at all-time low numbers, and government spending makes up more than 25% of our economy. The numbers are a dismal reminder that no one can overturn economic law, not even the largest government in the world. America's politicians have been on a spending spree since WWII and have financed it with the American taxpayers' money. Marrying a defective economics system that glorifies government spending with power hungry politicians that are looking for any excuse to spend our money is a recipe for disaster.

Why is it that every responsible American family must balance their budget monthly or run the risk of serious consequences, but our elected officials cannot seem to master this standard requirement?

In the United States, there are one hundred senators, 435 congressmen, one president, and nine Supreme Court justices. A total of 545 human beings out of the 300 million are directly, legally, morally, and individually responsible for the domestic problems that plague this country.

Are you telling me that in America, there are not 545 people who can learn to balance the budget and tell their constituents "no" when they have to? You cannot have the proverbial cake and eat it too. The government continues to spend billions of dollars more than it is taking in which makes it the least effectively run business in America. Yet I hear people all the time state, "What we need is more government involvement." Ok, let me get this straight. The government that cannot balance its own budget (even though it has the largest revenue stream) will now be teaching its techniques for success (failure) to the rest of the private economy? That is like going to a homeless shelter and assigning one of the unfortunates to teach his business acumen to the Chamber of Commerce.

We are systematically robbing our children of their birthright in an orgy of spending and irresponsibility. Americans need to demand responsibility in their government and find 545 people with the following skills and character: budgeting, ability to say no, integrity, principle centeredness, willing to confront reality, understand economic principles, historical perspective, vision casting, and leadership. I refuse to be part of the generation that sat by idly and allowed our great nation to spend itself into poverty! Every businessman is held responsible to the bottom line by the market and profit and loss. We must hold our politicians responsible for the bottom line. We can right this ship, but we need less rhetoric and more confronting of reality on the issues. Here are just a few suggestions.

1. A government amendment to balance the budget yearly. Leadership requires tough choices and without this amendment tough choices are put off by borrowing money and leaving a bigger problem to the next generation of leaders.
2. Return to a Gold standard or a hybrid system that only produces money when real value is produced. It is too tempting for politicians to artificially produce money and inflate when in a pinch. Real money is only a measurement of value produced, not something that can be printed by fiat.
3. Reduce our foreign commitment of troops. If countries desire us to be the police force for them, then they must foot the bill. Who exactly are our troops in Western Germany defending against? Isn't this an appendage from the Cold War? Can Germany not defend themselves at this point?

4. Reduce the influence of special interests in the voting process. The elected officials need to represent the voters, not the special interests. Until we can have elected officials that are not owned by special interests, real change will be slow in coming.

DAILY DISCIPLINES TO SUCCESS

Nearly every time I sit down with someone for the first time I am asked, "What is the secret to your leadership success?" Instead of giving a general response, I will give my specific daily disciplines to produce results. I encourage everyone to develop their own Daily Disciplines to build a successful life. It has been said that you determine your habits, and your habits determine your results. I strongly believe this and I am constantly evaluating my habits to ensure they are leading me towards my long term goals and dreams.

When Laurie and I mentor a couple, the first thing we are listening for are the habits that have been formed. What habits do you do on a daily basis? Did you think through these habits to build a successful life or are you aimlessly developing habits with no thought toward the results produced from them? Your answer to this will make all the difference.

Here are my Daily Disciplines to Success:

1. Prayer - When I wake up in the morning the first thing I want to do is turn my mind to my Lord and Savior. I am a Christian before anything else and I desire to start the day remembering Jesus Christ and what He has done for me. This keeps everything in perspective for me and no problem is ever bigger than Him. Pray to be filled with the Holy Spirit and let Him lead your life. Determine each day to do right and live a life that can be written in the clouds. Without character and principles, who will or should follow you? Start and end each day with Prayer.

2. Bible Reading – Start each day with some quiet time to read from the Bible. I personally like to read the New King James, but there are other great translations and many love the original King James. I read a couple of chapters from the Bible and follow up with *Matthew Henry's Abridged Bible Commentary*. Matthew Henry was a puritan who live in the 1600's, but his commentary is so needed in today's compromising age. I cannot express enough how much this commentary has helped me in developing my world view. I also read a couple of daily devotionals to focus me on all of my blessings. This habit ensures I keep an outlook of gratitude and keeps bitterness at bay.

3. Review/Plan Schedule – I like to make a morning cup of coffee and review the agenda for the day. During this time, I like to verify I am accomplishing the task in an effective and efficient manner. I know that relationships always come before tasks I think through my key relationships. I want to ensure we are moving in the right direction together. I ask myself, "Are the things I am doing today taking me towards or away from my long term goals and dreams?" I also keep another notebook handy to jot down any ideas I had while sleeping. Some of my best ideas come to me while I am waking up. This is my thinking time.

4. Praise & Encourage – My goal on every phone call is to address the subject matter for the phone call, but also to praise and encourage. We live in a world filled with discouragements and disappointments. Do not pile your criticisms and discouragements onto other people's backs. You will attract more bees with honey than vinegar. Do I address issues? Absolutely, but I sandwich any issues between genuine praise, encouragement, and thankfulness for their friendship and partnership. Make every phone call, personal contact, or e-mail/text a chance to praise and encourage. Think about this from your personal experiences. With whom do you enjoy spending time? All of us are attracted to encouragers and people who believe in us. If we are all attracted to this—why not develop the habits to become an encourager and believer in others? It has always puzzled me that the thing we like the most in others is

rarely developed in ourselves. EVERY great leader I know is a master of genuine praise and encouragement.

5. Exercise for 30 Minutes – I don't care if it is a brisk walk, working with weights, running, or whatever. Find something that will increase your heart rate that you will develop into a daily discipline. No matter how busy I am, I will at a minimum do push-ups and sit-ups before jumping in the shower. Develop a plan and have the discipline to follow through until it becomes a habit.

6. Listen to Leadership/Personal Development CDs - I believe strongly in the "University on Wheels" concept. How many hours do you spend behind the steering wheel? Listen to CD's and give yourself an education on leadership, attitude, and people skills. If I am in the car driving alone, I shut off my phone and turn on a CD. This is my time to develop so I can serve others better. In my opinion, this is the number one separator between the achievers and non-achievers. Make this a daily discipline!

7. Read from a good book - The subjects of leadership, history, economics, theology, philosophy, politics, etc. will make you a better conversationalist and build wisdom. You cannot live long enough to have the personal experiences necessary to win. Draw upon other successful people's lives and decide now to home-school yourself for life. Education is never ending and you are both the teacher and the student. What grade would you give yourself as a student? My good friend Charlie "Tremendous" Jones stated, "You will accomplish results in life based upon the books you read and the people you associate with." Develop the daily disciplines to ensure all of your relationships are healthy and moving you toward your long term goals and dreams. Reading books is a way of associating with the greatest minds of the ages and learning how they thought. I am who I am based upon the books I have read and the people with whom I have associated.

These are the basics that will propel anyone reading this to success. Progress is important and these Daily Disciplines will drive you toward your goals and dreams. The Daily Disciplines will help immensely.

If you don't like something change it; if you can't change it, change the way you think about it. - Mary Engelbreit

The only people who find what they are looking for in life are the fault finders. - Foster's Law

He who has so little knowledge of human nature as to seek happiness by changing anything but his own disposition will waste his life in fruitless efforts. - Samuel Johnson

Toughness is in the soul and spirit, not in muscles.
- Alex Karras

People seem not to see that their opinion of the world is also a confession of character. - Ralph Waldo Emerson

I have found that if you love life, life will love you back.
- Arthur Rubinstein

PARTIAL BIRTH ABORTIONS - THE CRIME AGAINST CONSCIENCE?

This discussion is designed to get people to think and examine their beliefs and values. We may disagree, but we can disagree respectfully as human beings with different thoughts on the issues. I feel our society loses when we lose the ability to dialogue and reason together. The topic of this discussion is an issue that is heated on both sides. We need cool heads to discuss rather than name-call on either side of the issue.

Our post-modern culture is good at casting aspersions on our forefathers for their hypocrisy. I will use just three examples to share my point. Have you ever heard any of the following?

1. Founding Fathers were hypocrites to say that all men were equal, but some had slaves.
2. Manifest Destiny was just a nice way of saying we are going to steal the land away from the Indians who could not stand against American firepower.
3. America needs to bring its troops home and let the countries that are defenseless against our firepower make their own decisions in government.

I believe each of these points has some validity and that we should discuss the ideals and the realities in each case. What concerns me is that our post-modern culture can clearly see the fault of past generations, but never seems to look inward at our own hearts. Jesus said, "Before you remove the speck from your brother's eye, remover the beam from your own eye." The Bible is clear that Christians should defend the defenseless, ensure justice to the weak against the strong, and stand up for those who cannot stand up for themselves.

The slaves during the American Revolution could not stand up for themselves and even though individual founding fathers did make stands, it took a Civil War to finally settle the slavery issue. The founding fathers had ideals, but could not implement them without risking the entire American experiment. Were they right or wrong to do so?

The Indians on our great plains could not stand up to the land hungry Americans moving west. Did individual American's attempt to enforce the Indian nations' rights? Yes, some did, but justice was trampled for expediency and Indians were herded off to plantations. Should America not have headed west at all? These are some of the great questions for ongoing dialogue that will be discussed for as long as people reason together.

The sovereignty of other countries is intervened by our powerful military and political machines. Does America have the right and responsibility to ensure justice for the oppressed around the world? These are more intelligent discussions with well reasoned argument on all sides. If America is threatened, do we have the right to intervene? There must be limits and principles applied to each situation.

"There is nothing new under the sun, only the history that you do not know."
- Harry Truman

The point is that we should always examine the past and the present to ensure our hearts are right and our minds are informed on these matters. The goal of studying history is to learn from the past so we can apply the right principles at the right time in the future. As Harry Truman said, "There is nothing new under the sun, only the history that you do not know."

I have said all of this to bring you to our post-modern culture's biggest hypocrisy and crime, in my opinion. How can we deftly point out the hypocrisy in our past and not blush with shame with our culture's stand on abortion? Isn't the American creed to stand up for those that are defenseless? Isn't it the blatant hypocrisy that gets our dander up when we see the double standards from our past of (free men and slavery, right to own property and land grabbing migrations, and (national sovereignty & empire building government)? How is it that we see their hypocrisy, but miss our own?

Can we truly say we are concerned about the welfare and rights of our defenseless brothers and sisters when we allow partial birth abortions? What more defenseless human being can there be than a baby in their mother's womb? I can see future generations looking back on this generation with disdain. They will mock our hypocrisy that we were concerned about the defenseless until it called for a personal sacrifice.

It has been said that integrity is not doing wrong, but character is doing right. You may not support partial birth abortions nor have had one and so that could be called integrity. But I would submit to you that character would go the next mile and defend in a Constitutional way the rights and the justice of our speechless and defenseless brothers and sisters. America's ideals have always stood for coming to the aid of the defenseless against injustice. Please consider your positions and examine your own heart. Do you have a double standard when it comes to judging the past and the present? Do you, like our forefathers, use misleading arguments to justify the hypocrisy? Like attempting to show that babies in the womb are not really human yet? Doesn't this sound frighteningly similar to the bogus argument about Africans not being fully human in an attempt to justify slavery? Does it sound like bogus arguments that Indians could not be fully civilized in an attempt to justify rapaciousness? Does it sound like fallacious arguments that the weaker countries need us to force upon them our form of government even though we would fight to the death to not allow a foreign power to do the same to us?

The Bible compels us to go beyond integrity and into character. I have made stands in my life that have cost me plenty. Money, friends, reputation must all be put on the line before you surrender your character and your principles. Can it be tough at times to stand for truth? Sure, but not as tough as looking in the mirror and knowing that you are a hypocrite. John Wooden said, "The softest pillow is a good conscience." May your pillow be soft tonight!

COMMUNICATION

Good communication makes people feel like they are valued by the leader. It helps people feel included. It makes sure they have the proper information to act upon and therefore their actions align with the direction and vision of the leader. Clear, timely communication also builds harmony and group spirit, as everyone is "on the same page" and can feel confident that they aren't wasting their time heading in the wrong direction.

There are several things to consider when communicating:

1. Clarity: it is important to be clear. As one of my professors used to say, "Be clear, be clear, be clear, and if all else fails, be clear!"
2. Timeliness: Get information and announcements out in plenty of time to be useful, calming, and relevant.
3. Informative and Complete: Irrelevant communication is worse than none at all. Incomplete communication looks hokey and kills trust in the leadership.
4. Honest: Nobody wants "spin." Be candid and straight in good news and bad.
5. Using Multiple Channels: With today's technologies, there are so many ways to communicate that leaders should have an easy job of it. Be sure and use multiple channels for getting your message out. One method reinforces another.
6. Personal: When you can, especially for important matters, use personal communication. Messengers, go-betweens, emails, and other "third-party" communication can actually be bad if the news is bad, of a critical nature, personal, or sensitive and possibly offensive to the recipient. Never use email or phone messages or texts to address behavioral issues or character

problems. For the important things, there is no substitute to direct communication.

7. Pervasive: There is nothing that creates division in an organization more than scattered, incomplete communication in which some parts of the organization are "in the know" while others aren't. Unless there is a specific reason to the contrary, spread information evenly and completely throughout your team.

8. The Law of Buy-In: Many communications should more naturally take in your biggest leaders and influencers first. This gives them a chance to " buy in" to the communication and also gives you, the leader, a chance at feedback before the communication reaches a wider audience. Ignore this one at your own peril.

In addition to this list, it always behooves a leader to become good at public speaking. The better a leader is at expressing himself verbally, in front of a group, the more credibility he is given and the more people are willing to follow. Many leaders could increase their effectiveness significantly if they could just improve their speaking ability. You have to be able to cast in order to cast a vision. To lead effectively you will have to learn to communicate effectively.

ANYONE COULD LEAD PERFECT PEOPLE

Leadership is with, for, and about people.

Leadership is with, for, and about people. One of the most important things for a leader to learn is how to deal with people.

I am amazed at the vast variety of people in our world. From different cultures, races, creeds, geographical locations, and a whole host of other orientations, the range of people out there is extremely diverse. This variety is amazing. It also poses challenges for any would-be leader who has to learn to engage with people with such differing outlooks, perspectives, beliefs, attitudes, and world-views.

Leaders not only have to get along with people, but they have to get along side people. They have to find a way to connect, to find common ground, to find something they can share, and ultimately to find a way to influence.

I am shocked when leaders complain about the people they lead, or act disappointed when people don't meet their expectations. Anyone could lead perfect people. But imperfect leaders are called to lead imperfect people. Leaders who expect their people to be perfect, or to be just like themselves, don't understand the realities of life OR leadership.

Leaders lead groups of imperfect people who squabble with each other, get their feelings hurt, get offended, hold grudges, play mental games, pout, fight with each other, are spiteful, selfish, and do unfair things. All this should be expected. The quest isn't for perfect people to lead, but for the leader to improve toward perfection so he or she can be more effective in leading people the way they actually are.

Don't get me wrong. The goal is to help people improve, grow, and change. There is no excuse for misbehavior and the selfishness I've just described. But leaders must deal in the reality that with people come challenges, and leaders must grow to be mature enough to endure it, thrive in that environment, and guide it all in a productive, vision-driven direction.

How do leaders do this seemingly impossible task? Primarily by loving their people. By having an accurate, realistic understanding of the fallen condition of humanity, and then being full of the love of Christ in dealing with those people, understanding that some of the same faults and shortcomings also reside within! This is done by having thick skin, being slow to anger, quick to forgive, and keeping one's eye on the bigger picture. It's also easier said than done.

THE LESSON OF INITIATIVE: THOMAS COCHRANE AND THE CAPTURE OF THE *GAMO*

One trait common to all leaders is initiative. Leaders don't have to be told to do something, they don't need managers above them, and they don't wait for the all lights to turn green before departing on a trip. Leaders take action, they take responsibility, and they don't take their time waiting and wondering if they should act. There is an old line that says there are three types of people in the world: those who make things happen, those who watch things happen, and those who wonder what happened. Leaders are the ones in the first group making things happen. A component in initiative is the courage to act. Another is decisiveness. Leaders display a willingness toward action, seeing what needs to be done and doing it without further delay. Initiative is not to be confused with recklessness. Instead, it is a mixture of a spirit of enterprise, courage, and competent decisiveness.

Englishman Thomas Cochrane's first command was the tiny brig misnamed the *Speedy*. It was actually quite slow and difficult to handle. But this fact hadn't stopped Cochrane and his crew from amassing an impressive string of victories, capturing scores of enemy vessels along Spain's Mediterranean coast. In fact, their successes had been so numerous that the crew of the Speedy was at about half strength, the remainder of the men having been sent off as "prize crews" responsible for sailing the captured crafts back to home ports. There were barely enough men left on board to sail the ship. The *Speedy* and its plucky commander had become more than a nuisance to the Spanish, whose trade had been significantly interrupted by the capture of nearly 50 ships in less than a year.

On the one year anniversary of his command, Cochrane was in pursuit of two Spanish gunboats that fled into the harbor of Barcelona. Apparently acting as decoys, the gun boats led the *Speedy* into the path of a thirty-two gun Spanish frigate named *El Gamo*, which had been sent out in search of Cochrane. The *Gamo* was four times the size of the *Speedy*, and had over three hundred sailors and marines on board compared to Cochrane's mere fifty-four. Whereas the *Speedy* had only fourteen guns, the *El Gamo* had thirty-two. The capability of the guns was all out of proportion as well, with the broadside of the *Gamo* being 190 pounds to the *Speedy's* 28 (a broadside was the total weight of shot capable of being fired from one side of a ship's guns and was a common measure of firepower).

Being too close to the larger ship to run for safety, Cochrane surprised his crew by deciding to turn and fight rather than surrender. According to biographer Donald Thomas, "The one factor in Cochrane's favor was the improbability of what he was about to do. The officers of the *Gamo* would never believe that anyone but a lunatic would try to attack them with a brig whose mastheads hardly reached much above their own quarterdeck." Cochrane sailed in close to windward (the side offering the advantage of the wind), and to cause confusion, he flew the American flag. Flying the colors of other countries, particularly a neutral like the United States, was a common ruse during the age of fighting sail. Nonetheless, it caused hesitation on the part of the *Gamo*. For the moment the menacing gun ports of the Spanish ship remained silent. Then Cochrane turned the *Speedy* and came around on the leeward side of the Spanish (giving the *Gamo* the wind advantage); another move designed to confuse. At this point, Cochrane quickly had his crew raise the British flag.

As the Speedy sailed closer at high speed, it somehow survived the first broadside of the larger ship. This was by design. Cochrane had surrendered the coveted "weather gauge" by giving the Spanish ship the windward position, and he purposely took the leeward side. Although battle maneuvers were more difficult from that side, it was also harder for a ship in the *Gamo's* position to fire at an enemy so close to leeward. This was because the wind heeled the ship over and shots were likely to go into the sea.

Cochrane told his men to hold their fire, and he instructed them to double-shot their guns. This meant they would have less of a firing range, but would spew forth twice the amount of projectiles and have the potential for causing much more destruction. "Grape" or "grapeshot" was a mixture of metal pieces and balls designed to scatter like a shotgun blast and inflict maximum damage to personnel and rigging. A double-shot dose of it, properly aimed, would be deadly to all in its path. It was risky to sail in close enough to use a double-shotted broadside, but it just might give the *Speedy* a chance.

A second broadside for the *Gamo* had no affect on the charging *Speedy*, which was approaching as though it meant to ram the bigger vessel. Then there was a crash as the masts and rigging of the two ships entangled upon impact. The *Gamo's* guns fired again, but the shot went over the heads of all aboard the tiny Speedy and only damaged sails and rigging. Finally, the *Speedy* aimed its comparatively little four-pounders as high as possible and fired. Because of the angle of the shots, upward and through the *Gamo's* gun ports, the effect was devastating. The flooring under some of the Spanish guns was blown upwards as the grapeshot scattered in its deadly patterns. The captain of the *Gamo* was killed instantly. The firing continued furiously from both sides, but because of the mismatch in size and gun position, the *Speedy* inflicted more damage.

Because of the ineffectiveness of their firing, soldiers aboard the *Gamo* made three attempts to "board" the *Speedy* and force a hand-to-hand fight. Each time, however, Cochrane would let the Spanish assemble for the jump across, then maneuver his ship to widen the gap of ocean between. Once perched in such a position, musket and small arms fire from the Speedy would wipe out the would-be attackers.

The fight continued in this manner for over an hour. Then, according to Cochrane, "The great disparity of force rendering it necessary to adopt some measure that might prove decisive, I resolved to board." His men, in disbelief over what they had so far achieved, enthusiastically responded to this practically suicidal order. Cochrane split his men into two groups, leaving only the ship's surgeon aboard and at the wheel. One group, with faces painted black for effect, went to the front and climbed aboard the *Gamo* from the bow. The other, led by Cochrane himself, climbed straight up the side of the Spanish ship. In the smoke, noise, and confusion, the Spanish were unnerved by the screaming black faces rushing at them from the front of their ship while they were engaged with attackers from the side as well.

In the tight quarters aboard the deck of the *Gamo*, the superior numbers of the Spanish could not be brought to full advantage. Even so, Cochrane was not out of surprises. In the middle of the melee, he called over to the only man left aboard the *Speedy* and instructed him, very loudly, to send the second wave of attackers. Somehow the recipient of the bogus order managed to contain his surprise, and pretended to comply with loud shouts and orders to sailors who didn't exist. Many of the Spanish apparently concluded that the *Speedy* had been packed with Marines and the whole battle had been a trap.

Next, someone noticed that the Spanish ensign was being lowered from the mast: the sign of surrender. But it wasn't the Spanish lowering it. Rather, it was one of Cochrane's men who had previously been instructed to do so at a proper point in the struggle. Before they could figure out that it was a trick, the disheartened Spanish, with their captain dead, laid down their weapons. Afraid the Spanish would discover how few had defeated them, Cochrane and his men were quick to shuttle the Spanish below decks, where they were held in position with the *Gamo's* two largest guns.

The tiny little *Speedy* proceeded to the British port in Minorca towing a prize ship four times its size. Donald Thomas wrote, "The *Gamo* should have been able to blow the *Speedy* out of the water before the British ship came near enough to fire a shot. The Spanish troops should have been able to overwhelm the depleted crew of the brig as soon as she came alongside. A man who was so foolish as to lead forty-eight seamen on board an enemy ship with a crew of more than three hundred ought to have found himself and his men prisoners within a few minutes." But it didn't happen that way. Instead, Cochrane had pulled off what Nathan Miller called "the finest single-ship action of the Napoleonic Wars."

ETERNAL
VIGILANCE

I picked up a newspaper on the plane this weekend. I wish I hadn't. After about a half hour with the thing, I was disgusted with how many false presuppositions permeated the articles. I was predominantly reading the finance pages, and here the assumptions made about economics were astounding. At one point in a financial book review the writer asked the book author whether Capitalism could still be considered a good system because of all the economic woes in our country these days. The author's response was something like, "Well, Socialism and Communism haven't been proven to work too well, either."

That's it? That's the defense given by a supposed 'expert' on economics? Where do they find these guys?

Blaming Capitalism for our bad economy is like saying a murder victim is at fault for consuming bullets. The economy would be just fine if someone, namely our over-reaching, meddlesome government, would stop torturing it to the point of near fatality. Talk about a water board!

Yet, such a ridiculous false presupposition was printed in an otherwise intelligent looking article. Why are so many (and let's just say it like it really is) false ideas allowed as though they are verified truths? Why do wrong assumptions stand as the foundation of arguments that are preposterous to begin with? Why do these (pronounced with nose in the air) intellectuals get away with being so incorrect?

I believe it's because most Americans don't really realize what's being said. Also, they are too busy trying to survive the bumps and bruises of their own lives to dig into the falsity of people who have nothing more to do than sit around and pontificate wrongly about things they've never actually done. All this while the "doers" are out doing it.

Our only defense against rampant falsity and its tragic consequences in our land is to make the time to get educated. A population that knows what's going on, that takes the time to peer behind the curtain at the scared man at the controls who is messing up our nation and trampling on its Constitution is the only way to guard against the loss of liberty.

I leave you with two of my favorite quotes from Thomas Jefferson:

"I predict future happiness for Americans if they can prevent the government from wasting the labors of the people under the pretense of taking care of them."

"The price of freedom is eternal vigilance."

CONFISCATION OR INCENTIVE

Understanding wealth and the truth of economic prosperity are critical to long-term survival of a nation or company or entrepreneur. Misplaced compassion, which taxes the engine of initiative and gives to the unproductive, sounds so good on its face. It also works very well at the voting booth. All one has to do is appeal to some group by using the power of either envy or greed, promising something for nothing, taken from others for their benefit, and explained under banners like "unfair," "equality of results," and "windfall profits." Those that propose such programs are either extremely ignorant of the truth of how economics work, or they know very well how things work but are willing to destroy the productive for the sake of their own power. In other words, they are either ignorant idealists with misplaced compassion, or cold-hearted power brokers rising on the destruction of the contributors.

These thoughts are important. Either the government is in charge of handling the wealth of a nation and distributing to whom it pleases in the moment, or the productive people and business owners who actually create the wealth in the first place are to be left in charge of the fruits of their own production. The more a nation moves in the former direction, the less freedom its people have. The more it moves in the latter direction, the more freedom its people have. And both tend to develop momentum in their continued direction. Governments that seize assets and distribute them to those who didn't have an initiative to produce them tend to grab more and more power over time, until the groups that were initially served by its redistribution are its next victims. On the other hand, when a government leaves its productive creators free to own their own first-fruits, incentive is increased and even more brilliant output results.

Once upon a time there was a little red hen who scratched about the barnyard until she uncovered some grains of wheat. She called her neighbors and said 'If we plant this wheat, we shall have bread to eat. Who will help me plant it?'

"Not I, " said the cow.

"Not I," said the duck.

"Not I," said the pig.

"Not I," said the goose.

"Then I will," said the little red hen. And she did. The wheat grew tall and ripened into golden grain. "Who will help me reap my wheat?" asked the little red hen.

"Not I," said the duck.

"Out of my classification," said the pig.

"I'd lose my seniority," said the cow.

"I'd lose my unemployment compensation," said the goose.

"Then I will," said the little red hen, and she did.

At last the time came to bake the bread. "Who will help me bake bread?" asked the little red hen.

"That would be overtime for me," said the cow.

"I'd lose my welfare benefits," said the duck.

"I'm a dropout and never learned how," said the pig.

"If I'm to be the only helper, that's discrimination," said the goose.

"Then I will," said the little red hen.

She baked five loaves and held them up for the neighbors to see. They all wanted some and, in fact, demanded a share. But the little red hen said, "No, I can eat the five loaves myself."

"Excess profits," cried the cow.

"Capitalist leech," screamed the duck.

"I demand equal rights," yelled the goose.

And the pig just grunted.

And they painted "unfair" picket signs and marched round and around the little red hen shouting obscenities.

When the government agent came, he said to the little red hen,

"You must not be greedy."
"But I earned the bread," said the little red hen.
"Exactly," said the agent. "That's the wonderful free enterprise system. Anyone in the barnyard can earn as much as he wants. But under our modern government regulations productive workers must divide their products with the idle."

And they lived happily ever after, including the little red hen, who smiled and clucked, "I am grateful, I am grateful." But her neighbors wondered why she never again baked any more bread.

(Author unknown, but very smart).

It is impossible for ideas to compete in the marketplace if no forum for their presentation is provided or available.
- Thomas Mann

THE POWER OF
AUDIO LEARNING

I will never forget the time I popped my first personal development audio cassette into my deck fifteen years ago. To say it had a major impact on my life would be an understatement. That one recording opened my eyes (and ears!) to a whole new world of self education. I became a junky. It developed into a habit that continues to this day: listening to the wisdom of others in an attempt to increase my own.

I really don't feel like this technique gets enough coverage in the world of self-development and leadership training. Most of what we learn will have to be intentional, and I can think of no better, more convenient, more osmotic method of doing that than getting in the habit of listening to educational recordings on a habitual basis; not just frequently, not once in a while, not when you feel like it, but constantly and with a fervor.

Listening to audio recordings of people who were in life where I wanted to be pushed me to learn what they knew. It pushed me to muster the courage to do what they had done. And it taught me to communicate and speak publicly myself.

I can remember things I heard over a decade ago on a recording like it was yesterday. I can quote speakers and authors by the hundreds. I can ask myself positive, goal-oriented, productive questions based upon principles I learned from listening with a hunger. And I have scores of techniques readily at my disposal, like a quiver full of arrows, based on things I heard over and over again on professional development audio recordings. I will forever be indebted to those individuals who unknowingly taught me a literal wealth of information.

What about you?

Are you giving yourself an abundant diet of positive, specific, edifying, uplifting, applicable, relevant, courage and attitude-building audio recordings? Do you listen to them every day? Is it a habit? Is it a love? Is it one of your favorite things to do? If not, you may be missing out on one of the most enjoyable and rewarding educations you could ever receive.

Just try it. Subscribe to whatever fits your needs the best (allow me to suggest LIFE Leadership's training materials, both specific and generic, available at lifeleadership.com). Listen to them over and over, not just for the entertainment value, but to make a deep impression on your thinking and attitude. I don't know how to overemphasize it, but I do know this: take away the educational listening I've done and you would take away most of what I have accomplished. It all arose in one way or another from the listening I did to my electronic mentors.

Do it. For your own sake. Begin listening and learning today. And if you have done this in the past but drifted away from it, get back at it! Get re-involved in the intentional improvement of your life. You will never regret it.

Think big thoughts but relish small pleasures.
- H. Jackson Brown, Jr.

Every thought is a seed. If you plant crab apples, don't count on harvesting Golden Delicious." - Bill Meyer

BIG GOVERNMENT
GOOSE KILLER

How did our government get to be as big as it is? How did we ever get to a place where we have millions of people casually (certainly not critically) thinking that the government can take care of them, that more and more taxes can be a good thing, and that bureaucrats can regulate economies better than free market forces?

History has given its answer very strongly to these theories, but they are harder to kill than the *Terminator* and The Agents from *The Matrix* put together.

"There is nothing so permanent as a temporary government program," said Ronald Reagan. And here we approach the root of the problem. What starts as a small program, perhaps well-intended extremely limited, promised only to apply to a select "few" (which is always a different set of people than those to which the appeal to support it is pandered; in the words of Congressman Bob McEwen, "When you rob Peter to pay Paul, you can always count on the enthusiastic support of Paul!"), and maybe even hailed as a temporary measure, undoubtedly becomes entrenched, spawns new agencies and administration, gets expanded (something called "bracket creep" in the military), and grows to an indestructible size.

> *"When you rob Peter to pay Paul, you can always count on the enthusiastic support of Paul!"*
> -Bob McEwen

Take for instance the U.S. Income Tax. In 1913 the 16th Amendment to the Constitution made income tax a permanent method of revenue collection for the U.S. government; something that had previously only been primarily a war-time expedient. Promises were made that it would only affect "the rich" (sound familiar?), and that it would always remain small (do any of you think that 24 to 38% is small?). In fact (and I think you'll notice the appeal to class warfare and envy in this statement, something else that should sound familiar) the income tax was sold to the people as a "Class tax" and not a "Mass tax." Although it is progressive, can anyone truly say it doesn't impact the masses? It impacts almost all of us.

What happened?

In the 1800s, Yale professor William Graham Sumner said "well-intentioned social progressives often coerced unwitting average citizens into funding dubious social projects." Andrew Mellon, secretary of the Treasury during three presidential administrations in the early nineteen-hundreds, wrote, "Any man of energy and initiative in this country can get what he wants out of life. But when initiative is crippled by legislation or by a tax system which denies him the right to receive a reasonable share of his earnings, then he will no longer exert himself and the country will be deprived of the energy on which its continued greatness depends."

In other words, if progressives in favor of big government and increased taxation are able to dupe enough people into following their programs, the goose that lays the golden eggs will eventually, pardon the pun, give up the goose. Taxing the engine of production that pulls the whole train along can only work to a certain extent. Eventually, the overtaxed engine can no longer pull against the resistance and all forward progress stops.

Do we really have to relive the 1930s all over again to prove that a big government and its interventions can kill an economy?

No one is free when others are oppressed. - Author Unknown

Nations grown corrupt love bondage more than liberty;
Bondage with ease than strenuous liberty." - John Milton

"Most people want security in this world, not liberty."
- H.L. Mencken

FRIENDSHIP:
THE ART OF THE HEART

Friendship is a lot like art; we find it difficult to define, but we know it when we see it, or more accurately, we know it when we feel it. The width and depth of friendships in a person's life can have a lot to do with overall happiness and sense of well-being. But a term so common that we all assume we know what it means may, for that reason, be worthy of a deeper look.

Some people have a lot of friends. Some have few or none. Some friendships last a long time, others are fleeting and only for a season. And while no one should or could define the depth and quantity of friendships for another, there is a certain amount and quality that is required for all of us as part of the overall picture of happiness and fulfillment in our lives. We ignore this truth at our own peril.

Friendships are a special kind of relationship where two people, for whatever reason, develop a bond. Perhaps they have something in common, or they enjoy an activity together, or they just seem to "click." Over time, the predictability, comfort level, and mutual gain from the relationship strengthens and the bond of friendship is formed. It requires nothing formal, nothing so much as even an admission that it exists, but it exists nonetheless. Friendships grow, as all good parents should know, on the truth that love is spelled "T-I-M-E." As time passes it allows the connections of friendship to strengthen. Memories are made, events are encountered together, and an overall environment of trust and predictability is fostered. There must be some degree of openness and honesty for anything real to develop. Unselfishness and some amount of mutual respect are also required. In the end, both parties must somehow be "served" by the connection for it to last.

Friendships, then, grow quite naturally out of a bond that develops between two people for their mutual enjoyment and gain. But friendship is not so clinical as all of that makes it sound. Real friendship is something quite special, something to be treasured, something to be respected and maintained and provided for over time. Real friendship can become one of the most enjoyable portions of our time on this earth.

How does one become a friend? How does one attract and maintain friends? Friendship is an art of the heart. The more you have a heart for other people, and the more you are able to express it in ways sincere and creative, the more people will be attracted to you on a level of friendship. I have been blessed with many deep and lasting friendships in my life. I attribute these to the Grace of God in bringing them into my life more than any ability or worthiness of my own. Nevertheless, I cherish them and seek to foster and strengthen them as if they were entirely my responsibility. These people are special, and they have provided so much for me over the years that I want to give back into their lives as well. In other words, I want to be worthy of their friendship.

A question we should consider is whether we are good at making friends? Are we the kind of people others are attracted to? Do others know that we care? Can we be counted on in a time of need? Is our heart right toward others? Do we have a heart for people? Are we unselfish and focused on others?

A good exercise is to make a mental list of the people in your life who you consider to be your closest friends. Then, consider who might put you on such a list!

You may like the results of this thought process, or you may not. But it would be wise for all of us, whether we feel successful in the arena of friendships or not, to make some careful assessments of our ability as artists on the canvas of friendship. We could all stand to pick up the brush of "service to others," or of "patience and understanding," or of "encouragement and expression of affection," or of "listening without judgment," and apply them to the relationships in our lives, remembering that the best way to gain a friend is to be a friend.

DREAM BIG. SERVE HARD.
LIVE LARGE.

"Our greatest fear should not be of failure, but of succeeding at something that doesn't really matter!" - D.L. Moody

So how is your life going?

Is it what you always wanted?

For most people, the answer to those two questions is not good. They somehow have worked hard for a chunk of their life only to end up some place they don't want to be. Not good, indeed.

Let's not even bother analyzing in this article how you got to be where you didn't want to be. We'll delay that until I'm feeling more philosophical. Instead, let's cut to the chase. If you don't want to be where you are (figuratively, and perhaps physically speaking, too), the question is, "Where DO you want to be?"

The answer to that question for most people, interestingly, is fuzzy! And therein lies the problem. If you don't know where you want to be, you sure as heck won't end up there.

So what's it look like; the life you've always wanted? What does it feel like? Who's in it? What do you do with your time? With whom do you serve, love, and laugh?

The key to answering these questions comes from knowing yourself. What has your Creator given you? What are you good at? What makes you feel rejuvenated and alive? What makes your adrenaline pump? Also, what stirs your soul, stokes your righteous anger, and brings out your courage? It is there, at THAT red X on your Life's Treasure Map, where you should start to dig.

It's your life. You only get one chance. Don't waste it doing something that you weren't built to do. Don't invest your life in some-

thing that doesn't matter.
Dream Big. Serve Hard. Live Large.

FALSE
PRESUPPOSITIONS

Socrates, the gadfly of Athens, said his wisdom came from knowing that he did not know all the answers. I find it interesting that so many scientists and academia behave as if they have all the answers. In the scientific field, absolute certainty is difficult to obtain since another experiment may prove your studies incomplete or outright wrong. I love the quote from F. A. Hayek that states, "Nothing is more securely lodged than the ignorance of the experts."

Have you ever wondered what ignorance might be lodged in our current beliefs in different fields of study? Imagine living before the Copernican revolution. The starting assumption was that the earth was the center of the solar system and it was dangerous to believe otherwise. Imagine the times previous to the germ theory in medicine. A doctor would work on cadavers and then deliver a baby without disinfecting or washing. Right ideas and wrong ideas both have consequences. If you begin with the wrong assumptions, it is very hard to arrive at the right answers.

Socrates' genius engulfed the idea of questioning your assumptions to protect yourself from securely lodging your ignorance. The goal of this book is not to tell you what to believe, but to help you question your assumptions. We must study the current dogma poured forth from the academia, media, and ruling authorities in order to truly think. I occasionally will get (hate filled) and (thinking empty) comments in response to some of my writings. This is most likely the result of the commenter being fearful of questioning his assumptions and thus losing the certainty of his ruling beliefs. With less than 40% of Americans *reading* even one entire book in a year, I am concerned that we will swallow whatever we are told from the so-called experts. My goal is to get people reading and thinking again. By providing access to different thoughts through articles, books and videos, perhaps we can turn the tide.

I have started a list of areas in which to discuss beginning assumptions. After each area I have described the current ruling dogma that is serving as the beginning assumption:

1. Economics – Ruling dogma is Keynesian
2. Science – Ruling dogma is Darwinism
3. Medical – Ruling dogma is prescription drugs
4. Political – Ruling dogma is democracy and the rule of 51%
5. Christian – Ruling dogma is post-modern theology
6. Philosophy – Ruling dogma is post-modern thought
7. Success – Ruling dogma is university education and a subsequent corporate job
8. Leadership - Ruling dogma is positional authority
9. Marriage - Ruling dogma is that love is something you feel, not something you do
10. Law - Ruling dogma is judicial activism
11. Education - Ruling dogma is centralized education

As I read the discussions on both sides of each of these issues, I am amused at how dogmatic the proponents of the above dogmas are in their viewpoint. What is there to fear in genuine discussion? False initial assumptions preclude people from rationally discussing or thinking through the actual situation. Thinking can be dangerous to the reigning assumptions, but I would argue it is much more dangerous to not think. There are very strong and significant, well-informed, historically supported presuppositions to supplant each of those listed above. Again, if we start with incorrect assumptions, we cannot get to truth.

Men fight for freedom, then they begin to accumulate laws to take it away from themselves." - Author Unknown

READING

Nearly all the noteworthy leaders throughout history have been big readers. Reading is the shortcut to successful thinking, the route to accurate perspective, and the doorway to knowledge. Reading can be fun and entertaining, enlightening and inspiring, and should always lead to a better understanding of our lives and the world we live in.

It is tragic that in our entertainment society we are losing our literary bent. From what I can tell, although every airport has a book store, and although Barnes and Noble and Amazon seem to be doing fine on-line, there is a decline in the habit of reading. With video games, movies, television, Internet, sports, traffic, hobbies, organizations, kid's sports and activities, longer working hours, and that endless list of errands that need to be run, we seem to have very little time for simply reading. I suggest, however, that it is important for us to *make* time to read. As busy as people get, it seems that they always find a way to do the things they want to do. Reading should be a priority that is worthy of a spot in our busy schedule.

Think about how much of our daily living is just thrashing against the current. It doesn't carry us forward toward our goals and dreams, nor does it even hit on our priorities. In fact, a major percentage of our lives is *spent* and not *invested*. But reading is an investment. It is important. It should be a priority in itself. It jump-starts our brain and reminds us that we were created for more than just the daily grind.

Have you read the classics? Do you have at least a working knowledge of some of the writings from the greatest minds of history? Do you read from several different genre? Have you had a book that has touched you deeply or awakened you to something grand?

Let me suggest that you make it a priority to increase the quantity and quality of reading in your life. Make it part of your daily schedule; something that becomes habitual. The more you do it, the more you'll like it, until you find yourself yearning for the next break in your schedule where you can enthrall your mind once more. There is a whole world in the pages of great books. Go discover it for yourself!

To be upset over what you don't have is to waste what you do have. - Ken S. Keyes, Jr.

Defeat is not bitter unless you swallow it. - Joe Clark

The only disability in life is a bad attitude. - Scott Hamilton

HELP
OTHERS WIN

One of the most important things to understand about leadership is that it is not about YOU. People who crave what leadership can provide, thinking that this entails perks, power, position and status, are really not fit for the position. Reluctant leaders, a term that at first seems like an oxymoron (as opposed to the regular, run-of-the-mill moron), is actually one of the prerequisites for the job.

History is full of people who were reluctant to assume the mantle of command, but through that very humility, contributed in enormous ways to their cause. Usually, the injustice, cause, and/or vision is so compelling to the leader that he or she cannot help but get involved and start shaping events in that direction.

> *"The higher up you go, the more you need to make other people winners and not make it about winning yourself."*
> - Marshall Goldsmith

What leaders discover is that leadership is not about themselves, perks, power, or position, but rather about empowering and serving others. The better the leader, the more he or she serves others. Empowerment sounds like a corporate buzzword, but is actually extremely important. As author Marshall Goldsmith states, "The higher up you go, the more you need to make other people winners and not make it about winning yourself."

Remember: the world's biggest and best leaders make other people into winners. That is what we attempted to explain with the Five Levels of Influence in our *Launching a Leadership Revolution* book. The higher level leaders do more and more to make others effective.

To determine how well you, as a leader, are doing in this area, ask yourself the questions: How much did I deposit into the lives of others today? What did I do specifically to add to their capabilities, opportunities, and belief systems that can help them move on as leaders and winners? How are the people around me doing in their leadership development? Who can I help win? How?

Be mindful of this requirement in the world of leadership. Don't ever forget that leadership is about turning others into winners, and take some positive steps in that direction each day!

Lead on!

COURAGE OF YOUR CONVICTIONS OR COWARDICE OF YOUR COMFORTS

I love the definition of courage given by Robert Morrisette: "Courage is not the absence of fear, but the perception that there is something far more important at stake." I could not have said it better myself if I took the next year to try.

"Courage is not the absence of fear, but the perception that there is something far more important at stake."
- Robert Morrisette

Courage is not the strength inside of you as much as the strength of your convictions. Courage is really a matter of what you are focusing on. Study any person of courage that you know. You will find that what drives him or her is a conviction that is worth any cost. Without this conviction you will not pay the price. Cowards have no convictions worth dying for and that is why they never truly live. If you are focused on God's Glory then you can endure many setbacks, failures and heartaches because you know there is something far more important at stake. If you are focused on what is happening to you then you will shrink back from God's Glory to self-comfort. Lives are defined by those special moments when we must choose between comforts and convictions. I pray you choose wisely.

SOME FIGHTS ARE
WORTH MAKING

Author Alan Axelrod recently wrote an interesting sidebar about founding father John Adams:

"'For my part,' John Adams remarked, 'there was not a moment during the Revolution when I would not have given everything I ever possessed for a restoration of the state of things before the contest began.' This is perhaps the most extraordinary confession of the entire war. It tells us that debate, doubt, and even regret were active at the very core of the Revolution, that the idea of reconciliation was at least as powerful as the idea of breaking away, and that words and ideas would be as important in shaping the conflict as powder and lead. If King George III and the conservatives in Parliament had been even a little more conciliatory, or if men like Thomas Paine had been a little less persuasive, it is likely that the Revolution would have been averted or settled amicably."

We read and talk all the time about the brave defiance to tyranny the colonies exhibited during the Revolution, we see how they risked their "lives, their fortunes, and their sacred honor" to stand up for what was right, and we know that they fought a long and bloody war and ultimately survived to birth a free nation. But it is easy to forget that they attempted, repeatedly, to offer the "olive branch" to King George III and Parliament, we forget that they also had a yearning, deep down in their breasts, for peace and harmony.

Why was the natural inclination for peace and appeasement not heeded? Why was the wish to avert armed conflict not satisfied? In my view, it was because God had other plans. Although it would have been nice to have averted war and found a way to maintain peace, it wouldn't have been right. Although it would have been easier to keep the status quo and preserve tranquility, it wouldn't have been just. And because these people were willing to sacrifice to stand firm for what was right, a great and mighty result was accomplished that has benefited hundreds of millions, living in a free society, ever since.

This brings us to, perhaps, one of the most difficult things for good-hearted, peace-loving people to understand: Without justice, there can be no peace.

Who among us wouldn't desire peace over war? Who among us wouldn't wish tranquility over violence? Who among us wouldn't ignore some small offense for maintenance of the status quo? Who among us, in the heat of battle and at the height of sacrifice, wouldn't, like John Adams before us, wish to turn back the clock and return to simpler, quieter times?

This reminds me of a scene from the movie *Lord of the Rings*, in which Frodo becomes weary and scared of his unsolicited burden of carrying the ring back to Mordor. In speaking to Gandalph, Frodo basically says he wishes he'd never been given the ring to carry. Gandalph's answer is beautiful, and to me, entirely correct. Paraphrasing, Gandalph basically says, "That's how everyone feels when they find themselves in a position of great responsibility (where their peace and affluence have been wrecked by a fight for justice), the only question is, what are you going to do with the time you've been given?"

Why does Gandalph answer Frodo by talking about time? Because how we use our time goes straight to the heart of the matter. Frodo was longing for bygone days of peace and solitude. Frodo had grown weary in well-doing. But Gandalph reminded him that he still had a choice. He could continue his fight for good, his pursuit of justice against the dark forces of evil, or he could return to his solitude and peace. The choice was clear, Frodo could either serve his sense of justice, or he could serve his desire for peace. But

PRACTICE YOUR CRAFT

The more I study successful people, the more I am reminded of the obvious. Whether it is someone in business, sports, or whatever, the best at their professions are those who are "into what they are in."

I am not sure why our society looks upon successful people at the top of their "game" and concludes that they are lucky, or that they should be criticized and picked apart. If someone achieves something great the conclusion seems to be that that person had breaks others didn't have or cheated to get there. This tendency runs right along with the trends in our national politics that feed off envy and class warfare. "If they had less, we'd have more." "It's not fair." "Equal opportunity is not enough. We want equal results."

The real answer is that the successful person was burning for success and achievement while the unsuccessful was doing less productive things or behaving in less focused ways. Michael Jordan is almost universally considered the greatest basketball player of all time, yet he is also legendary for his incredible work ethic, drive and determination. Even at the top, perhaps especially at the top, he worked out consistently, intensely, and purposefully. Tom Brady has achieved what few quarterbacks ever have, yet he is also known as the hardest working player in training and in study on every team on which he's played. Do I even need to mention Tiger Woods and his robot-like practice schedule? Andrew Carnegie was notoriously hard working, even as one of the world's richest men. Bill Gates long tenure atop the software industry was marked by persistent attentiveness and tireless workdays. Stephen King's prolific writings came not only from a gifted and imaginative mind, but from his habitual work habits in which he held himself responsible for writing a certain amount of words each day.

So many lessons we try to teach our children still apply to us. None can be more true than the lesson of practice. Practice, practice, practice. Doing what you do makes you better at what you do. Being at it, early and late, consistently and persistently, is what builds greatness. Put your whole self in, again, and again, and again. Be into what you're in. And do it over the long term.

Does it sound like a lot of work? It is. Does it sound like it might not be worth it? That's an individual choice. Does it sound like greatness requires fanaticism? It does. It also requires focus and time. That's just the way it works. The laws of success are not open to negotiation. Pay the price or don't. The choice is up to each of us. But when someone else makes the choice for greatness in their chosen area, we should neither envy their rewards, nor down-play their achievement by calling them "lucky" or "talented."

"Heights by great men reached and kept were not obtained by sudden flight but, while their companions slept, they were toiling upward in the night."
- Longfellow

In the words of Longfellow: "Heights by great men reached and kept were not obtained by sudden flight but, while their companions slept, they were toiling upward in the night."

If you aren't fired with enthusiasm, you will be fired with enthusiasm. - Vince Lombardi

I don't like that man. I must get to know him better.
- Abraham Lincoln

There are no menial jobs, only menial attitudes.
- William J. Bennett

RELATIONSHIPS

If you are going to be a leader, you are going to be in the business of building and maintaining relationships. For some people, this is a nearly automatic thing, but for many, it is less than natural. Both types of people, however, should and must learn to make this critical area of leadership a priority.

In a sense, a leader's life is a collection of the relationships he or she develops. The value, depth, synergy, permanence, and harmony of those relationship will literally make or break a leader. With this being not only true, but hopefully obvious, why is it that so many would-be leaders either fail terribly here or seem to pay this topic no serious regard? Why is it that relationships are so callously thrown away, eroded, neglected, or abused? I believe the answer is a combination of the following:

1. Ignorance
2. Pride
3. Ego
4. Selfishness
5. Greed

Among others, this list reads like the typical litany of human sinful failings. Considering ignorance: perhaps leaders don't realize how important their web of lifetime relationships is to their success and lasting legacy. This is inexcusable. And for those reading this article, it is no longer a possibility. You have been warned.

The rest are much more serious. Leaders who allow these and other failings to get in the way of initiating, constructing, and maintaining relationships will cause both themselves and others a lot of pain. As the saying goes, "Hurting people hurt people." I am consistently amazed at the amount of score keeping, gossiping, pouting, indignant anger, the preference of being "right" rather than loving, and rank coarseness that is exhibited by leaders which wrecks their relationships. It is as if the would-be leader thinks that as long as he or she is "right," any amount of responding behavior by them is justified. WRONG. When discussing these failings with them, I usually hear responses like, "Yes, but (the other person) did such and such." Okay, but what the other person does is irrelevant.

What?

Let me say it again. What the other person does is irrelevant. Why? There are several reasons. First of all is that the Lord will hold you accountable for YOUR behavior alone. Secondly, we know right off the top that none of us is perfect, and that we are all fallen and sinful creatures, so why should someone else's failings and shortcomings justify a similar reaction from us? In the words of my mother many times over when I was a child, "Two wrongs don't make a right!" But the third reason is the point of this article: what is important here is the RELATIONSHIP.

For a leader, building relationships must take priority over being right, winning, getting even, venting anger, righting wrongs, and the like. (Now don't get me wrong: I am not saying that there aren't times when an injustice is actually being done by someone, especially when it is being done to someone else, and must be addressed for someone's protection). But yet I see many people willing to throw away months, and sometimes even years, of investment in a relationship because someone got mad, felt justified in their outburst of anger, or otherwise was willing to trash a relationship for something of lesser value.

An excellent leader would rather give a little bit here and there than tarnish or take away from a relationship. *An excellent leader "dies to self"* An excellent leader would rather apologize, even if he or she wasn't sure they were actually at fault, than take a "withdrawal" from a relationship. An excellent leader "dies to self" rather than angling for personal gain at the expense of others.

And let me issue a warning, here, for those who understand these principles and apply them only to people they think can bring them gain: leaders love everyone and treat them with respect even if a person can't do anything for them in return. Remember, it's how you treat "the least of these" that Christ said he would count as how you treated Him! This is certainly a leadership principle to fully grasp!

So handle ALL your relationships with tender-loving care. Be gentle, kind, caring, loving, long-suffering, honest, open, genuine, and as Christ-like as you possibly can. And when you fall short, apologize quickly and express your respect for the person and your commitment to the relationship. Do as author Stephen Covey recommends by considering your relationship with each person to be a bank account into which you either make deposits or withdrawals, working consistently to maintain and grow a positive balance. And never forget, your job as a leader is to build relationships. Ignore this at your own peril.

DREARIES VS. LEADERS

In Dante's *Divine Comedy,* in *Canto III,* Dante is guided by Virgil, the Roman poet of antiquity, to the gates of Hell. The first beings they meet on this perilous journey are a group of lost souls called the "Drearies," who linger around Hell's gate. As Dante writes, they are "those who lived without blame or praise." Author Thomas Cahill calls them "whining wraiths who never truly lived at all, the lukewarm, who are 'as hateful to God as to his enemies,' the people no one claims."

To me the Drearies are the very opposite of leaders. They lived on earth for a number of years, ate food, labored at things, and then died. Their lives are entirely forgotten because they stood for nothing, fought for nothing, risked nothing, attempted nothing, and died as nothings. And, at least in Dante's imagination, their eternal life will be comprised of endlessly more of the same.

Leaders are passionate beings. They attack the status quo, sometimes at great peril to their own peace and well-being. But leaders can do no less. They live while they are alive. Their internal light shines bright for accomplishment, contribution, service, impact, making a difference, and leaving a legacy. Leaders burn with a purpose to fulfill and never feel quite right when not in alignment with that purpose.

Tragically, though, many people fall into the trap of the Drearies. They don't do much wrong, but they don't do much right either. In fact, they don't do much at all. And if they do, they simply dabble. Pastor Robert L. Dickie was given some advice early in his ministry from an experienced and stately gentleman: "Don't be a dabbler." He says that thought always stuck with him and has served to keep him focused on his biggest priorities.

Why are so many people complacent? Why do so many dabble? Why do so many frit away their days in nothingness and wake

146

up at the end of it all and wonder, "what if?" I wish I had the answers to these and all similar questions. But I do know that life lived fully is better than life simply lived out. We shouldn't tip-toe through life trying to get to death safely. We should stand and make a difference with the gifts God has given us. Through prayer, counsel, scripture, dream-building, service to others, and meditation, we should search for our life's purpose and then chase after it with everything we've got. You will never regret the time you spent giving your all to a worthy purpose.

So find it.

Give to it.

Live it.

NOT ALL REVOLUTIONS
ARE EQUAL

To those only slightly familiar with the history of revolutions in the world, the word itself, 'revolution,' has a positive connotation. Most Americans are drawn back to the dawn of our country with fond admiration and respect; as it should be. Despite the fact that we entitled one of our books, *Launching a Leadership Revolution* (our intention being to conjure the good meanings of 'revolution'), all revolutions aren't good. Many, many revolutions through history were bloody, unjust, horrific affairs ending in tyranny. Only a few, despite near universal propaganda to the contrary, have ever amounted to much more than 'the mob taking over.'

Take for instance the so-called French Revolution of 1789. What began in high-sounding platitudes (at first blush similar to those of the American colonials) ended in mass murder and crowd-manic-hysteria. What was the difference? As author Fareed Zakaria wrote, "France placed the state above society, democracy above constitutionalism, and equality above liberty."

First, community and society are more important than the government. In fact, the government exists to serve society, not the other way around.

Second, democracy cannot predominate over the 'rule of law' (restraints placed on the majority so they don't infringe upon minorities).

Third, individual liberty must be protected against encroachment and/or infringement by other individuals, groups, or even the government itself. The U.S. Constitution is supposed to be a set of chains to bind the government from taking advantage of its people, not the other way around. There can never be equality of results among people; only equality of opportunity and treatment under law. People will always perform at different levels, seek different callings, and work at different objectives and accomplishments. Ensuring 'equality of results' is simply another way of embodying the concepts of Communism, and the earth has almost 100 million corpses in its soil to prove that the pipe dream of Karl Marx and his ilk has been tried and found wanting (actually, it has been tried and found murdering)!

Strange, isn't it, how things get flipped around when we are not diligent? The Constitution is supposed to protect the people from the government, but many today assume the opposite. The 'separation of church and state' concept (which, by the way, is not embodied in America's founding documents, but comes rather from a letter from Thomas Jefferson to a friend), was originally meant to keep the government from establishing its own religion and forcing it upon the people; it never even referred to the concept of keeping people from bringing their religion into the government! Laws meant to protects individual freedoms increasingly get interpreted by the court system in ways that limit (and often eliminate) the freedoms of individuals.

So not all revolutions are good. Not all good sounding phrases work out in actual practice. One sure gauge is to compare any politician, platform, movement, group, or sound bite against two staggeringly different templates:

The first: The United States of America's "Life, Liberty, and the Pursuit of Happiness."

The second: France's "Liberty, Equality, Fraternity."

One leads to freedom. The other to death. It really is that simple.

OVERCOMING CRITICISM

There is an interesting process involving how new ideas meet resistance and then overcome it. Achieving anything of lasting value means you will go against the grain and think outside existing patterns. Your ideas will go through four phases if you persist. First, they will be ignored. Second, they will be laughed at. Third, they will be fought. Fourth, they will win. This is why it takes courage and backbone to do anything new. Here are some favorite quotes on overcoming criticism.

"It is not the critic who counts; not the man who points out how the strong man stumbles, or where the doer of deeds could have done them better. The credit belongs to the man who is actually in the arena, whose face is marred by dust and sweat and blood, who strives valiantly; who errs and comes short again and again; because there is not effort without error and shortcomings; but who does actually strive to do the deed; who knows the great enthusiasm, the great devotion, who spends himself in a worthy cause, who at the best knows in the end the triumph of high achievement and who at the worst, if he fails, at least he fails while daring greatly. So that his place shall never be with those cold and timid souls who know neither victory nor defeat."
- Theodore Roosevelt

"When we judge or criticize another person, it says nothing about that person; it merely says something about our own need to be critical."
- Anonymous

150

"Any fool can criticize, condemn, and complain but it takes character and self control to be understanding and forgiving."
- Dale Carnegie

"Any fool can criticize, condemn and complain and most fools do."
- Benjamin Franklin

"He has a right to criticize, who has a heart to help."
- Abraham Lincoln

"If you have no will to change it, you have no right to criticize it."
- Anonymous

"One mustn't criticize other people on grounds where he can't stand perpendicular himself."
- Mark Twain

"Ridicule is generally made use of to laugh men out of virtue and good sense, by attacking everything praiseworthy in human life."
- Joseph Addison

"Critics are like eunuchs in a harem; they know how it's done, they've seen it done every day, but they're unable to do it themselves."
- Brendan Francis Behan

"Let the refining and improving of your own life keep you so busy that you have little time to criticize others."
- H. Jackson Brown

"It is better to be making the news than taking it; to be an actor rather than a critic."
- Sir Winston Leonard Spenser Churchill

"I criticize by creation - not by finding fault."
- Marcus Tullius Cicero

"A successful person is one who can lay a firm foundation with the bricks that others throw at him or her."
– David Brinkley

"The man who is anybody and who does anything is surely going to be criticized, vilified, and misunderstood. This is part of the penalty for greatness, and every man understands, too, that it is no proof of greatness."
– Elbert Hubbard

"To avoid criticism, do nothing, say nothing, be nothing."
– Elbert Hubbard

"Criticism is prejudice made plausible."
- H. L. Mencken

"We are never more discontented with others than when we are discontented with ourselves."
– Henri Frederic Amiel

"You can't let praise or criticism get to you. It's a weakness to get caught up in either one."
– John Wooden

THE POWER OF GOAL SETTING

Goal setting is something everyone has heard of and very few actually do. Of those of us that practice it, or try to, on a regular basis, many of us fall into some traps along the way. But goal setting done properly can invigorate and produce incredible results.

Don't be like the average person out there who isn't striving for anything, who lets life simply parade on by, who doesn't exercise his or her gifts to the fullest exertion, and realizes toward the end of his or her life that most of it has passed. Goal setting is a way to keep positive pressure on one's self. It is a way to make sure we are living while we are alive. And it is actually quite fun, believe it or not!

Goal setting is a way to keep positive pressure on one's self.

Here are some guidelines to proper goal setting:

1. Goals should be realistic but challenging: a goal should be something that you actually believe you can accomplish, but at the same time, it should put a little fear into you that it will require significant effort on your part to accomplish.
2. Goals should be specific: General goals have no power to inspire. Specific goals leave you no place to hide.
3. Goals should be written down and displayed where you can't forget about them: a goal not written down is simply a wish. Once written, however, a goal becomes "official" and remains on display to keep you in the game.
4. Goals should be measurable: There is no sense in setting a goal if you have no concrete way of measuring your progress toward that goal. Make sure goals are measurable, and check your

153

progress regularly.

5. Goals should be in line with your overall purpose: One of the biggest challenges in life is not succeeding, but succeeding at something that really matters! Don't get sucked into setting goals for accomplishment in areas that are not your heart's desire. You only have one life, God built you for a specific purpose, figure out that purpose and pursue it with all you've got! THEN set goals in that area! Remember, only do what only you were built to do. Leave everyone else's agenda to them!

6. Goals should stand alone: What I mean by this is that some people set too many goals. They set goals in different areas, at different levels, and before very long at all, they are confused by them all. This is not the way to set goals. The secret of success is to focus. One dominant, overriding goal will produce creativity and action. So keep it simple and singular.

7. Goals should be short-term enough to put pressure on you today: A "someday" goal will not work, and is nothing more than a fantasy. A goal must put you in positive tension today, or it is not functioning properly. If you have set your goal out there far enough that you think, "Well, I can get started on that tomorrow and still have time to accomplish it," then you've set it too far out on the calendar.

8. Goals should have a specific date of accomplishment: This goes with number 7 above. Make sure you have a finish line marked on your calendar.

There is much more to goal setting, but for me, these are the high points. Follow these, and you'll be on your way to achievement and significance. Neglect this technique, and you'll waste days, if not years, that you'll never get back. What is your overriding goal right now? If you don't have one, set it quickly and get after it. The clock is ticking!

To be wronged is nothing unless you continue to remember it. - Confucius

I don't think of all the misery but of the beauty that still remains. - Anne Frank

HARD WORK

I will never understand how decadence can be considered 'cool,' nor how laziness can seek justification as rebellion. How can ingratitude be disguised as victimization, or cynicism as intelligence? These are the bastardizations prevalent in our society today. And they all have something in common: they are equally pathetic.

Honor goes to the man and/or woman who works mightily toward honorable aims. There is, has been, and always will be dignity in hard work. One of success's biggest secrets is no secret at all: "Those who toil upward in the night" will beat the less committed nearly every time.

Just as predictable as the fruits of hard work is that when work is meaningful it doesn't even feel like work. The man or woman giving full effort toward meaningful endeavors gets 'caught up' in it, 'wrapped up' in it, engulfed, fanatical. They grow to love it. Predictably, this is also when the video game players, sports junkies (okay, I'm a little guilty here), passivists, lazy, unmotivated, un-goal-directed, un-purposeful bystanders will start to air their 'concerns.' "We're worried about you," they'll say, sometimes sincerely, sometimes not. "You can't keep such crazy hours." "Slow down, enjoy your life." But such statement may as well be offered up in a foreign language. To the truly inspired, they will fall on deaf ears.

Try to stop Tiger Woods from pursuing his goals. Make Eli Manning stop throwing touchdowns. Go back in time and convince Michael Jordon to refrain from practicing so hard. Greatness has no answer for such obstruction, besides pity. The 'great ones' look at those who mock them, those who try to stop them, or even those who admire them, and feel sorry that these others 'don't get it.' They must be perplexed how people can fail to understand the joy and fulfillment that comes from giving one's all to a calling for which one was designed.

Don't ever shy away from hard work. Chase it down and honor it with your full intensity. Apply yourself mightily in the direction of something meaningful and honorable. You may not be understood, but you will not be disappointed.

The greatest discovery of my generation is that a human being can alter his life by altering his attitudes. - William James

Could we change our attitude, we should not only see life differently, but life itself would come to be different.
- Katherine Mansfield

Enjoy the little things, for one day you may look back and realize they were the big things. - Robert Brault

WHAT IS THE UPSIDE OF ADVERSITY?

Napoleon Hill said, "Behind every adversity is the seed of an equal or greater benefit." That is easy to say, but much harder to live during times of adversity. What makes some people champions is their willingness to endure adversity that would debilitate a lesser person. Many have the opportunities and talents, but few have the perseverance to win. Learning to maintain a winning attitude during setbacks is a key attribute of every leader.

> *Behind every adversity is the seed of an equal or greater benefit.*
> -Napoleon Hill

Leaders learn to draw on their inside character to rise above the adversity, while similar troubling times sink the pretenders.

I count it one of my greatest blessings to have gone through so many adversities in life. Adversity doesn't develop character as much as it reveals character. A fast starter is not necessarily a champion until they finish what they started. It's not until you are knocked flat by adversities that your character is revealed. I don't wish challenges on anyone, but I know that mental muscles are strengthened through resistance. It isn't what happens to you in life that counts as much as how you handle what happens to you in life. Challenges bring clarity of purpose.

Read the history of the greatest leaders. Every leader has defining moments of adversity that reveal something extra inside of them. There is no Winston Churchill of WWII fame without the Churchill who 'failed' in WWI. Churchill was blamed for the failed Gallipoli invasion and banished from government. Winston had to endure criticism and scorn during his desert experience after WWI that prepared him for his destiny in WWII. Winston's stand against Hitler flowed from his convictions solidified during his adversities. Great Britain had its 'finest hour' because Churchill previously had his personal 'finest hour.' Internal victories always precede external ones.

A leader is like a horse; they're not useful until they're broken. Brokenness does not mean being a loser or having no spine. But it does mean that you are through with your personal ego. Only when you move from personal ego to a team ego that focuses on others will true leadership begin. Leaders help others overcome adversity to achieve their dreams. Leadership is not for the weak of heart, as adversity is a given for any real leader. Leaders must face and defeat their personal Goliath before leading others into adversity. A leader's example gives the courage to others to face and defeat their personal Goliath. By facing adversity, your leadership example inspired them to leadership. What an ennobling and rewarding experience and the true joy of leadership!

How do you view adversities in your life? Are you getting bitter or better from the adversity? Change your perspective and learn the lessons of perseverance. Leaders must expect their Goliath and confront them. The next time you are dealing with adversity, remember that adversity carries with it the seed of an equal or greater benefit. Now is the time to plant that seed and reap your leadership harvest.

THE LEADERSHIP
TRACTOR PULL

The older I become the more I learn, and that's a good thing. However, some things I learn I really didn't want to learn. I believe its instructional that the fall of the human race occurred with the eating of the fruit from the tree of the knowledge of good and evil. As it is quoted, "With much wisdom comes much sorrow."

But then, I overstate things a bit. Perhaps the best way to explain the concept is to relate the illustration of a tractor pull. Somewhere, way back in my teenage years I attended a county fair. At that fair was featured a tractor pull. The process was fascinating. Grease-monkey gear-heads from all around turned out to display their souped-up horsepower fire wagons, and pit them against each other in the tractor pull competition. If you've never seen one yourself, here's how it works: a tractor starts out pulling a heavy drag sled across dirt or gravel. As the sled slides forward, a blade gradually digs deeper and deeper into the ground, thereby steadily increasing the resistance that must be overcome by the tractor. Eventually, the resistance becomes too much for even the most capable tractor, and the progress is marked in the dirt for all the other competitors to surpass.

I know you've already seen where I'm going with this. When I study history, as is one of my passions, I can almost see each stand-out leader as a tractor pulling against the sled, struggling against opposing forces with all his might. At the end of the leader's life historians mark his spot of forward progress and assess and compare his performance. Not a very inspiring sight, but accurate to a degree, I'm sure. As one ascends the ladder of success, rising higher and higher, responsibility also increases, sometimes even disproportionally (a drag sled out of control). As I've often said, "Leaders often carry an unfair load." Unfair to an average performer, perhaps, but not to the leader. That is because the bright side of the increase of resistance and responsibility is an increase in influence and results. Significance and fulfillment also increase exponentially.

Leaders often carry an unfair load.

This is where my illustration breaks down a bit. There is no way a tractor struggling along, belching out smoke, straining harder and harder in a futile battle can be a totally accurate picture of leadership because it doesn't illustrate the increasing rewards gained by the leader for his or her efforts. Further, and perhaps most importantly, the leader has the capability to do something along the way that the tractor cannot do: increase their horsepower! While a tractor in a pull shows up for the competition with all it's got and can gain no more, a leader can always grow in the process!

A leader can read, learn from experience, mentor with someone, and grow stronger because of the struggle. This surprising and almost intimidating fact is extremely inspirational. Truly, there is no defeating a leader who is committed. No matter what happens, what failure, setbacks, or obstacles confront them, they continue to morph into something bigger, better, and stronger than they were before. To be certain, this type of development is only accomplished by the rarest type of person. But then again, leadership at that level is uncommon, commitment of that magnitude is unusual. It's available to everyone, but exhibited by only a few. This is why leaders are such interesting people and why their stories are so popular. There is something in the human spirit that loves achievement, overcoming of obstacles, and beating the long odds.

Every time a leader overcomes challenges and rises to fight again she is stepping closer to fulfilling her destiny and maximizing her potential. The key is to improve and grow faster than the resistance increases. If not, the leader's progress peaks right at that level. The track officials might as well mark it in the sand because the pull is over.

So each of us should make sure we are doing everything we can to grow in and through the process of struggling upward toward our destinies. Remember, we can't take our same old self into a bright new future, if we did, we would simply darken it! Instead, we need to be made better and stronger through the resistance so that we can handle the higher level as well as the rewards. Why? Because we are tractors, and tractors were built to pull.

SYMBOLS OF THE OPPRESSION OF LIBERTY

Between the fall of the Roman Empire in the fifth century A.D. and the formation of "country states" by the beginning of the crusades some five hundred plus years later, an interesting symbol began dotting the landscape of Europe: the castle.

As an amateur admirer of architecture and the designer of my own home, I have long been intrigued by the design, beauty, and function of castles. On a tour of England once I developed a near fanatical interest in ramparts, portcullises, loopholes, dungeons, keeps, and the like. Every bit an instrument of war as much as shelter, of projected power as much as protection, castles throughout the period demonstrated enormous diversity and creativity. Over the years their construction evolved from wood to stone to humongous masonry structures designed to repel the assaults of siege machines such as catapults and trebuchets.

Architecture aside, however, castles were also representative of the sociological change of the times. Power and the rule of law had been centralized in Rome, with local vassal kings and imperial governors selected by the emperor. Once Roman power had been transplanted eastward to Constantinople and the remaining authority in Rome disintegrated, the landscape was open to ambitious princes and dukes. From time to time would-be Caesars attempted to knit the ancient empire back together in all its glory, but none of these efforts ever had the scale or durability of what had gone before. Eventually, it became obvious that might ruled the day and slaughter and conquest was the secret to advancement. As hundreds of princes scattered across Europe made claims to noble blood lines, they constructed castles on every possible hilltop and cliff to project their hegemony. With banditry and violence

162

everywhere, peasants needed protection and were herded into villages within retreatable distance to the local castle. Where once a people had been (at least to some degree) "free," now they were transformed into "serfs" in one of the largest protection rackets the world has ever seen (the Mafia has nothing on these guys).

The castle, then, became the symbol of the oppression of ancient liberties. The peasantry was not ignorant to what was happening; they came to resent the castellans' grasping of power at their own expense. There were some notable revolts, such as the attacks on the Harzburg castle in Saxony, but there was little the poorly armed, unorganized peasantry could do. If there had ever been a time when the common European could have prevented the putting over of himself of a castellated lord, that time had passed before anyone was aware of it. In the final analysis, the last remnants of freedom for the peasants had disappeared with the rule of Roman law.

It is a shame that in our own day the encroachments on our freedoms aren't as visible as the castles of the Dark Ages. We, too, like the peasants of old, are losing our freedoms as the rule of law gradually disappears. The structures that are being erected to control and mollify us are not ones of stone and mason, but of government bureaucracy and majority rule. And just like the serfs of Europe who longed for the extinct pax romana (Peace of Rome), we too may awake one day yearning for the good old days of Republican, representative government.

Most historians appear to agree that the peasantry of Europe was largely powerless to stop the onset of feudalism. Common people were not sufficiently informed or knowledgeable of the changes creeping in around them, and they never organized in a fashion that would blunt the trends effectively. In our society today, we may be faced with the same combination. The average American is uninformed about the erosion of his freedoms, and has at his disposal little chance to make a difference. In a two party political system that offers very little difference (in terms of actual governance, if not the rhetoric) to the voter, in a government controlled by special interest lobbies, what can the common citizen, concerned as they may be about his future and that of his children, actually do? This is the question, more than any other, that I am asked the most frequently.

For starters, we can become educated ourselves about what kind of government we are supposed to have, and what we actually are experiencing now. Next, we can share this information with others, disseminating materials, websites, video clips, and (in short), the truth to everyone we can. Thirdly, get active in the political process. Vote. Write your representatives. Join organizations that believe in what you believe.

There is a lot we can do. We don't have to be serfs, watching the construction of a castle with fear and trembling. These are not the Dark Ages. Nor, while we have anything to say about it, will it be said of our future, either!

FIND YOUR
AUTHENTIC SWING

One of my favorite movies of all time is *The Legend of Bagger Vance.* Not that I'm such a great golfer (in fact, I'm not a golfer at all, although my boys are recruiting me), but the lessons, principles, and cinematography (good job, Robert Redford) are excellent.

The precept is that a young man, who was a gifted golfer as a youth, went to World War I and came back messed up. He couldn't golf anymore, feeling responsible for the death of his comrades, and unable to clear his head. Ten years later a mysterious caddy named Bagger Vance shows up to work him through his challenges. The young golfer, called Captain Juna, said he had lost his swing. Bagger Vance shows him what an "authentic swing" is by referring him to his competitors. Although his competitors had radically different styles, they were both effective at the game because they played it their way, their authentic way, doing what they were born to do.

Captain Juna goes through many ups and downs during the big three day tournament. Sometimes he catches a break and does well for a while, but then his reaction to it is arrogance and cockiness. Then he messes up horribly and gets dejected and loses confidence, whining that he shouldn't be playing at all. Finally, when it is almost too late for Captain Juna to have a chance in the competition, Bagger Vance pulls him aside and says, "It's time." Juna resists at first, but Bagger Vance presses the point, telling Juna that it is time to move on with his life, time to drop the baggage of the past, time to find his authentic swing and do what he was born to do.

I love this movie because I see its application so much in the development of leaders and in helping people achieve success. Rarely

165

do I meet people who lack the ability to become great leaders and achieve great things. Rather, I meet people who have been through some wars in their life and it has left their heads messed up. They feel responsible (as they may be) for damages in their life, and they deem themselves not worthy of accomplishing anything. It's as if they have already died and are waiting to make it official. Add to this the negative messages the world sends them about "not trying too hard," not wasting time trying to achieve greatness, not risking anything, not getting their "hopes up," and you can see that their self-talk, mixed with the world's "mediocrity talk," is a breeding ground for insignificance and unhappiness. But just like Bagger Vance, I get to tell people that "it's time," it's time to find their authentic swing, that thing that they were born with the skills to do, that thing that makes them come alive, that thing that they know, deep down inside, that they are supposed to achieve. This usually involves reminding them that they were born with the seeds of greatness inside. That God makes people and he doesn't make mistakes. That they were born for something meaningful, even if the world doesn't agree with it.

Bagger Vance has a term he calls being "in the field." It's when a person is fully authentic, doing what they are supposed to do, using their God-given gifts the way they were intended. It's as if everything comes together at moments like that, and it doesn't matter what the critics say, what the world says, or even what your relatives say, when you discover your authentic calling and are living right smack dab in the middle of it, you are "in the field," and there is no better feeling in the world!

Sadly, almost nobody that we run into in our daily lives is living with anywhere near this kind of purpose or authenticity. How tragic. A person is born with all the hopes and possibilities that life has before them, then somehow just wastes it in days of insignificance and misalignment.

Don't let that happen to you. I don't care how old you are, what "wars" you've been through to this point, it is only up to you how you live your life. It has to look right to you, and you only. You were born and built for a purpose, and it's not too late. In fact, IT'S TIME.

WHY PEOPLE STAY
IN COMMUNITY

It is an interesting study to find out why people stick with a certain organization, company, business plan, etc. In recent corporate-speak, this concept has come to be know as "community." Building communities is one of the most spectacular, rewarding, fun, frustrating, interesting, mysterious, heart-warming, infuriating, pleasurable experiences. This is because people are people, and they come in all shapes and sizes (figuratively as well as physically). Through life's journey, it is people that bring meaning and richness to life, and it is people who also bring trial and tribulation. Some you love, and some you, well, you get the picture.

Building communities is all about surfing through the various waves of human interaction in a positive, lifting manner, learning the skills of knitting together relationships. It is also about heart and caring and perseverance in the name of brotherly love. This might all sound a bit weird for a corporate setting, but the basic fundamentals of successful human interaction are the same everywhere.

What becomes funny is when corporations, managers, or so-called leaders think they have other means to keep people in community. The first thing amateur leaders think of is compensation. If people were simply paid better, they would be happier within an organization and more productive, sticking around to enjoy the benefits. Others seem to think that programs and slogans will get it done. Others have proposed work environment solutions, or leadership styles, or ongoing training, or trendy techniques. Still others rely on corporate "spin," telling their people how great the organization is over and over and thinking that the people are actually buying into the misrepresentations. But as Abraham Lin-

167

coln said, "you can fool some of the people all the time, and all of the people some of the time, but you can't fool all of the people all of the time (paraphrased)." Spin becomes the things a company tells its employees and the public that neither believe to begin with. The saddest in the corporate world try intimidation, dogmatic dominance, litigation, red tape, and entrapment to keep their people in community. Stories abound of employees or business associates being mistreated as a way to try to get them to stay in a community.

Author Marshall Goldsmith reports the findings of an extensive study that gets to the bottom of human interactions and what actually keeps people in community. According to Goldsmith, it boils down to three things:

1. Meaning and happiness, NOW
2. "I like the people here"
3. "I can follow my dreams here."

If any of these are violated, a person will check out of the community; first emotionally, and then physically. In fact, the best way to see how an organization is doing at building and maintaining community is to see how many are leaving. The leading indicator and predictor of the organization's future is to see how many people haven't yet left physically but have "left the building" emotionally.

IT'S ALL IN
YOUR THINKING

Learning to discipline your attitude is not just a nice skill to have as a leader - it is an essential element that determines whether you lead situations or situations lead you. Negative situations and thoughts will hit you daily if you are leading at any level. The key is how you think about each situation. I look at negative situations as an opportunity to fix them and strengthen my understanding of the people, processes, and failure modes that created the issue. Avoiding problems will not help them go away. Denying that your thinking is off is like denying you smell after three days without a shower.

How long do you allow your *thinking to be stinking* before you address it? How do you address it? The right way is to go to your mentor and tell them how you are thinking. See if he or she would think the same way, and if not, how would he or she think about it. In a mentoring role, I spend a majority of my time reframing people's thinking about their situation. Here is the key principle:

IT IS NOT THE SITUATION ITSELF THAT IS THE MOST IM-PORTANT ASPECT - IT'S HOW YOU ARE THINKING ABOUT THE SITUATION THAT IS MOST IMPORTANT!

I have seen nearly identical situations hit different couples and watched one shrivel and shrink into victims because of their circumstances. I have watched others in the same set of circumstances grow and develop into the leaders to handle the situation. Every leader has learned to discipline his thinking to have a victory over his circumstances.

Learning to discipline your thinking is a daily habit that must be developed by listening, reading, and mentoring. I refuse to let a day go by in my life where I am not reading a good book to sharpen my thinking. I cannot afford to go more than a few minutes with *stinking thinking*. If I haven't corrected my thinking in ten minutes, then I am on the phone seeking help. I shake my head at the people that would say, "Well I don't want to bother my mentor." Is this person's thought process really as follows: "My thinking is off, so instead of calling and addressing it, I will continue to stink and rub off my stink on my team, family, or anybody else who can't solve the problem. Leaders are constantly checking their own attitude and redirecting the thinking towards an empowering solution. Refuse to play the part of a victim. Leaders cannot be leaders and victims at the same time.

> *Leaders are constantly checking their own attitude and redirecting the thinking towards an empowering solution.*

Which hat are you wearing? If you place the victim hat on you will find you are jealous and envious of the success of others. A leader responds with the attitude of, "If they can do it then I can do it!" A victim responds by justifying why he hasn't done it and attempts to minimize the accomplishment of others. This is very sad. Instead of working to grow themselves, they choose to stew in their own rotten juice. The worst of the victims seek out others who look and act like victims because misery loves company.

The only known anti-dote to this victim disease is a healthy dose of learning and positive action. The best way to read someone's mind is through their actions. If they are not moving towards their goal they have adopted a victim mindset, no matter what they claim!

Always ensure that your thinking is leading you towards your goals and dreams. For me, any thinking that justifies why I am not where I want to be is ruthlessly removed from my train of thought. This is what I mean by *disciplined thinking*. The principle is that you will never rise above your level of thinking! The only limiting factor someone will have in their life will be their own thinking! A leader will quickly recognize this and set goals for his personal leaning and accomplishment, followed by goals for his team.

I am a leader and will think, act, and teach leadership to everyone I can. How about you? Are you ready to lead? Of course, there
are plenty of victim spots available at no cost, requiring no thinking, and gaining no results. The choice is yours. As for me and my
family, we choose leadership.

A FUNDAMENTAL CHANGE IN THINKING

They were raised during the Great Depression and were therefore hardened by struggle and want. When the world needed them to intervene to help stop Fascism they were ready and able, tough enough and of sufficient character to pass the test. Some have taken to calling them the "Greatest Generation." From everything I can tell, they have earned the name.

During the course of World War II, 35,946 United States military pilots lost their lives in *accidents*. In just one year, 1943, 850 died while on home soil training to fly just one airplane, the B-24 bomber. But that's just one category within one country. Experts now cite the total number of World War II deaths at around 72 million!

Deaths are one statistic, but suffering is another category that statistics can't really measure. How many families lost loved ones? How many homes were destroyed? How many starved, became orphaned, or became refugees? Can anyone truly count the cost of such a calamitous time?

In America, the World War II generation came home and tried plugging back into normal lives. Only what they found was anything but normal. The catastrophies around the world depleted the globe of its industry, and the United States quickly filled the void. As a result, the economy boomed. Times got very good. Luxuries were invented almost daily. Conveniences abounded. The children of the Greatest Generation had quite a different life from their parents, and when "their war" came (Viet Nam), the Hippie movement began. Politics and just-war theories aside, it is unarguable that the mindset of the sixties generation was radically different from that of the forties. America had somehow fundamentally changed.

This new generation then grew up and took their turn at the helm of society. The most radical among them, those whose thoughts and world-view were as far as possible away from those of the Greatest Generation, tended to fill positions in universities, journalism, the arts, Hollywood, government, and education. In large part, they became the thought-shapers for the next generation. We are now reaping the harvest of that sewing.

The Founding Fathers of America believed very strongly in education. In fact, some of them went so far as to say that our Republic would not stand if not run by an educated populace. If you read their works closely, however, you will discover that education for education's sake isn't what they were talking about. They weren't concerned with the *amount* of education, but the *quality of the thinking* that resulted from a proper education. In other words, they knew that if the American people ever got to where they didn't understand the fundamentals of freedom, they would lose it.

> *If a nation expects to be ignorant and free, in a state of civilization, it expects what never was and never will be.*
> - Thomas Jefferson

In an earlier writing I gave a paraphrase from Thomas Jefferson. The actual quote is, "If a nation expects to be ignorant and free, in a state of civilization, it expects what never was and never will be."

We now have a voting public that has drifted so far away from the basic understandings of the principles of freedom understood by our founders that we are in the red zone. Even the father of Communism, Karl Marx, was smart enough to see what would happen. He said, "Democracy cannot long survive, people will vote themselves all the money in the treasury." Only he was off the mark. In the United States (which was founded as a Republic but is now called a Democracy by most of its people), the "people" have figured out how to vote themselves Trillions of dollars that aren't even in the treasury! And we've elected politicians who are only too happy to keep the printing presses running to feed our sloth.

We have somehow crafted a national mindset largely opposed to the thought processes that shaped our nation and supported the heroics of the Greatest Generation. We have indoctrinated almost two generations with a weak, socialistic mindset. If mis-education got us into this mess, proper education can get us out of it. We must once again teach the truth of freedom and develop an understanding of its principles. We still have a choice, but time is running out.

In the words of Sage Francis, "The waterline is rising, and all we do is stand there."

GIVE THEM SOMETHING
TO SHOUT ABOUT

There is a comfortable, easy lifestyle available to anyone who wants it. You can have peace and even affluence, if you wish. You can pass through your days without anyone bothering you too awful much, and can slip through the pages of history without so much as an enemy.

What is this lifestyle, you say? It's the life lived by someone who doesn't really live it. It's the life lived by someone who never takes a stand, who won't take a position, who takes no risks and colors inside the lines their whole life. For many people, I fear this sounds a little too attractive. Just find some nice, peaceful, noncontroversial way to get through your life and make it to death safely.

But that's not what leaders do. Leaders attack the status quo. They can't stand things the way they found them, and they not only *want* to make a change, they realize that they *have* to make a change.

Leaders attack the status quo.

If this is true of a leader, then automatically true at the same time is the fact that a leader will take criticism. Try to help people, and someone will say you are doing it for personal gain. Try to achieve something, and be criticized for having ambition. Try to leave a legacy, and someone will call you an egomaniac. Try to do something unconventional, and someone will call you a rebel. Try giving to a great cause, and someone will say your cause is unjust.

When I study history, this is one of its aspects that fascinates and inspires me the most. In fact, there is almost a proportional ratio that the greater the leader the greater the criticism and vile opposition he or she had to face. This gets missed sometimes. We

175

know George Washington led the colonial army during the American Revolutionary war, and we remember him by stiff paintings and busts, but it is easy to forget that for eight years an opposing army was doing everything they could to KILL him and his soldiers! We know Winston Churchill stood defiantly during Britain's "finest hour," but it is easy to forget that one of humanities worst characters did everything in his power to destroy not only Churchill, but the very population that put him in power.

Michelangelo is arguably the best artist to ever walk the planet, but he was criticized violently in his day. Ulysses S. Grant was the general that finally understood the method by which the Union Army in the north could defeat the Confederacy in the south, but his critics hurled massive bile his way for his conduct of the war and his alleged drinking problem. Martin Luther King was assassinated for striving peacefully toward civil rights, and even with a strong legacy people still like to whisper about his extramarital activity. Pastors who preach the message of the gospel of Christ are vilified for being offensive. Christ himself was crucified on a cross.

So don't be surprised by the unfair opposition you will face if you take a stand for anything. And by the way, the more aligned your position is with Biblical truth and the Judeo-Christian world-view, the more violent will be the opposition. It's just the way it works. Christ said it would be this way.

The only alternative? Do nothing, Be nothing, and Stand for nothing.

Personally, I'd rather give them something to shout about!

Whenever you fall, pick something up. - Oswald Avery

Success is due less to ability than to zeal. - Charles Buxton

We awaken in others the same attitude of mind we hold toward them. - Elbert Hubbard

HEART OF FIRE AND SPIRIT OF HONOR

In the novel *Ireland*, the wise woman told Ronan that, "What a poem needs by way of a good home is a heart of fire and a spirit of honor. Poems won't come to rest in a place of baseness. No self-respecting poem would think of entering a soul of perfidy."

While this may be insightful as pertains to poems, I believe that it is even more pertinent to leaders.

Recent events have served as a type of litmus test for me regarding leaders. Tumultuous times reveal character and true motivations more than any other. And during these events I have seen revealed the deficiencies in leadership of either "Hearts of Fire" or "Spirits of Honor."

I personally believe that leadership is made up of *both* a "Heart of Fire" *and* a "Spirit of Honor." A Heart of Fire represents Force, and a Spirit of Honor represents Light. My observations are that there are many, many leaders who are filled with a Heart of Fire, raring to go, pushing their way to the front, coura-

> *A Heart of Fire represents Force, and a Spirit of Honor represents Light.*

geous and boisterous, climbing toward their goals. There are also many people, though in the leadership category, I think, perhaps a smaller number, who are Spirits of Honor, decent, kind, nice, selfless, concerned about others, and focused upon doing what is right, simply because it is right, even if it is personally costly. But rare is the leader who possesses both. Great leaders need both a Heart of Fire and a Spirit of Honor; in other words, both Force and Light.

Too many leaders are all Force and not enough Light. And this brings me to my theme: excellent leaders balance the two. Excellent leaders are just as concerned about doing what's right, being honorable, honest, and a force for good as they are attaining their own goals and successes. Excellent leaders conduct themselves nobly, with grace and humility, and are more concerned with being a contributor to the overall team, the overall good, the overall legacy, than they are about their personal gain. Excellent leaders make decisions that are costly simply because they are right. Excellent leaders risk personal gain because they have a higher standard of righteous conduct that overrules selfish ambitions. I could wax on, but I won't. Everybody reading this knows what I am talking about: HONOR.

What would the world be like if more of its "leaders" were at least as concerned with being honorable as they are with being successful? What would the business world be like if its "leaders" were slower to maneuver for their own advantage and quicker to consider what is most honorable to do in a given situation?

Successful people are a dime a dozen. Gaining wealth is really not a big deal, and usually, not much of an achievement. Fame is a hollow promise laced with misery. The only thing that really lasts for a leader is his or her conduct, decency, selflessness, service to others, sacrifice, and honor. THAT is the legacy of a leader.

As with poems, leadership won't come to rest in a place of baseness. No self-respecting legacy would think of entering a soul of perfidy.

Lead on. And do it with honor, or don't do it at all.

CYNICISM AND THE FALSE BELIEF IN PROGRESS

In the smash-hit movie *Titanic* a few years ago, moviemakers combined fiction with history. As usual, the history wasn't exactly accurate. Tellingly, though, was the way in which the actual history was tweaked.

Most viewers of the film will remember the scene when the first class passengers rushed aboard the lifeboats. Only through the efforts of tough men with clubs was it even possible to get the women and children aboard the boats first. Terrible. Unthinkable. Unfair. Also: untrue.

We like it when our political misconceptions are reinforced. Popular media wouldn't be so popular if it didn't pander to our high opinion of ourselves and our society by feeding us what we want. That particular scene in the movie gratified viewers by showing them how unfair things were in the past compared to today's enlightened and egalitarian times. It also played right along with loathing 'the rich,' something common in political discourse today.

What actually happened was that the men aboard nearly unanimously adhered to the chivalric notion of 'women and children first,' and they did so in an orderly, heroic fashion. According to author Fareed Zakaria:

"In first class, every child was saved, as were all but 5 (of 144) women, 3 of whom chose to die with their husbands. By contrast, 70 percent of the men in first class perished. In second class, which was also inhabited by rich professional types, 80 percent of the women were saved but 90 percent of the men drowned. The men on the first-class list of the Titanic virtually made up the Forbes 400 of the time. John

179

Jacob Astor, reputedly the richest man in America at the time, is said to have fought his way to a boat, put his wife in it, and then, refusing to take a seat, stepped back and waved her goodbye. Benjamin Guggenheim similarly declined a seat, yielding his place to a woman, asking only that she convey a message home: 'Tell my wife . . . I played the game out straight and to the end. No woman shall be left aboard this ship because Ben Guggenheim was a coward.' In other words, some of the most powerful men in the world adhered to an unwritten code of honor - even though it meant certain death. The movie makers altered the story for good reason: no one would believe it today."

Sad, really, that 'no one would believe it today.' So go ahead Hollywood, change history to suit the assumptions of your audience. Reinforce their ignorance and biases for the sake of entertainment.

We live in cynical times when it is hard for many to believe that there were ages before ours that had honor, codes of conduct, and self-sacrificial service as standards of success every bit as important as material trappings and fame. We fall into the assumption that society progresses steadily upward simply because that is how technology appears to proceed. But just as nostalgia for bygone days is a bit naive and oversimplified, so too should we beware that when pushing forward with false assumptions bred of cynicism we leave something behind.

What if we could mix the honor of yesterday with the advances of today? What if chivalry grew as fast as computing power? These are things leaders need to think about, because with everything new comes the threat of leaving something good behind.

IF WE HAD LESS, WOULD WE DO MORE?

I had the opportunity over the weekend to hear a fascinating presentation from Erik Weihenmayer, the blind mountain climber who sumitted not only Mt. Everest, but all the other tallest peaks on the planet. Weihenmayer and his team of twenty-one members set a world record by having nineteen of them make the summit.

What was more incredible than Weihenmayer's feats of conquest, however, was the class and heart he displayed, without effort, on stage. I have rarely heard anyone speak so highly of teammates and the accomplishments and assistance of others. Weihenmayer was a master of giving credit away and shining the spotlight elsewhere. For a blind man to reach the top of the tallest mountain in the world, a team was definitely necessary. No one could have been more appreciative of their team than Weihenmayer; no sighted person could have had more of a twinkle in his eye.

As I listened to the captivating details of Weihenmayer's climbs, it occurred to me that the spark of something I caught in Weihenmayer's character came from two things central to his existence that are not to be found in the lives of most people I meet:

1. Weihenmayer was doing exactly what he was meant to do with his life, living in the center of God's purpose for him, and
2. He was doing it with all of his (dis)ability.

The pictures and film clips that he showed demonstrated these two facets of Weihenmayer's life very clearly to me. He was living his life in "the zone".

These observations set me to wondering. Why is it that so many people, given perhaps more physical blessings than someone like Weihenmayer, do so much less with their lives? Why do most people waste their days without ever seeking that purpose for which they were built? Why don't people take the risks to pursue what their God-given talents and passions point them towards? Then I happened upon the question: If we had been blessed with less, would we be accomplishing more?

Sure, Erik Weihenmayer has an obvious physical disability. But everyone, including Weihenmayer, has mental "disabilities." We are all limited by pride, ego, fear, lack of confidence, laziness, passivity, indifference, and the desire for comfort. Perhaps Weihenmayer became good at overcoming his limitations because he was forced to do so in the case of his lost eyesight. The same mental toughness he developed to overcome his physical disability may have become supremely instructive in how to overcome his mental disabilities.

I took great lessons away from Weihenmayer's talk. I realized how important a team is to individual success, and I learned from a master how to share credit and lift up others. I felt ashamed that I hadn't sacrificed more of myself toward my purpose, and I understood, for the hundredth time, that life in the zone is the only place to really live. It's when we have the guts to push ourselves to the limit, to surpass all edges of comfort and familiarity, to step out far on the ledge, to force our bodies into submission to our minds, that we will maximize all the potential God put inside us. Anything less is cowardice and lack of gratitude for our blessings. Anything less would suggest that we had been given too much.

"We plant seeds that will flower as results in our lives, so best to remove the weeds of anger, avarice, envy and doubt."
- Dorothy Day

"I am an optimist. It does not seem too much use being anything else." - Winston Churchill

LEADERSHIP CONDUCT: THE WORLD IS WATCHING

Class, character, honor, integrity, discipline, consistency, dependability, selflessness, and servant-hood are watchwords for anyone serious about being a leader. The conduct of a leader springs from the character of the leader. In other words, what's inside eventually comes out.

In the area of dealing with people, it is a short-term proposition, at best, and dishonest, at the worst, for anyone to simply learn people skills but disregard a heart change. It's a lot like putting a new dress on an old skeleton, lipstick on a pig, lacquer on a dirt clod, etc. Too many times people misunderstand the true change of heart that accompanies leadership growth for techniques and skills that are simply "on the surface."

Even so, I am still shocked from time to time at the lack of basic people skills from would-be leaders. Inappropriate tone of voice, quickness to be offended, grudge carrying, pouting, gossiping, being critical of others, arrogance, off-color remarks, negativity, complaining, criticizing, condemning, and the like are all too common from people who should know better. If these symptoms are prevalent, what does that say about what is on the inside? Where there is smoke, there is usually fire. The tree is known by its fruits.

Excellent leaders are very concerned for how they come across in their dealings with others. All the ones I know are sincerely humble, selfless, longsuffering, patient, kind, loving, forgiving, and self-effacing. Their tone of voice is smooth and kind, their eyes are focused and unwavering, their spirit is soft and other-focused, and their priorities are eternal instead of temporal. We would all do well to model this behavior.

But beyond the behavior lies the issues of the heart. Reading

183

good books, studying the scriptures, listening to positive and educational recordings, and attending meetings and conferences all should be used toward the purpose of an ever-growing heart. We should be prayerful for the Holy Spirit to invade our lives and produce a massive heart change within us. We should be mindful of our legacy, the impact we have on each and every person with whom we come into contact, and we should make our every interaction as positive and uplifting as possible. After all, the way we live our life might be the only sermon someone gets to hear. I particularly like the quote: "Whenever I am with someone, I want to treat them as well as if it were my last time seeing them. But at the same time, I want to treat them as if they will be important in my life forever." That is not only beautiful, but correct. Isn't that how the Bible basically commands us to behave as regards our neighbors?

We should be prayerful for the Holy Spirit to invade our lives and produce a massive heart change within us.

We can all grow in the area of our behavior towards and with other people. But most importantly, we need to grow on the inside. Our conduct as leaders matters. Right or wrong, people make judgments about a lot of things based on how they see us behave. They make inferences about our family, our upbringing, our faith, our God, our business, and our character based upon what they see us do. As the saying goes, "What you do speaks so loudly what you say I cannot hear."

So go for a heart change. And while you're at it, take the time to treat others with class and respect. The world is watching.

JUNKETS ON THE SHIP OF STATE

In 1927 a group of intellectuals set sail on an ocean liner for Europe and Asia. The overall objective of their trip was to gather information about the great Bolshevik experiment in Russia. Two of these men were Stuart Chase and F.J. Schlink, the founders of *Consumer Reports* magazine. Another was a peace activist named Roger Baldwin who had founded the American Civil Liberties Union (ACLU). Union men, magazine writers, and of course, college professors, made up the rest of the band.

Taking a trip to a foreign land in search of confirmation for one's progressive ideals may sound naive to our modern ears. In fact, such trips are now passé, and even expected of America's "elite" intellectuals. Who from that era doesn't remember Jane Fonda's trip to Viet Nam, or more recently Jimmy Carter's visit with Fidel Castro in the early 2000's, or even Brad Pitt and Angelina Jolie in the Middle East?

I love international travel. Foreign cultures, cuisines, geography, history, and especially the people are fascinating and wonderful. I highly recommend international experience to anyone as a fundamental part of their education. There is very little one can do to learn so much so fast, get large doses of a different culture, and the ever-popular-but-still-true broadening of one's horizons. I was fortunate enough to live for an entire season in East Asia and learned some language, forged some lifelong friendships, and gained invaluable lessons.

Things are different when such trips are taken for the purpose of confirming already held misconceptions, however. Under such circumstances, learning can't help but be hampered. This is because the lesson begins with stubbornly held and unexamined assumptions. Observations serve to confirm opinions instead of leading one to truth. For the distinguished passengers on the trip to Russia in 1927, Stalin began rounding people up, shipping them off to the gulags, and executing them even as the intellectuals sailed home with stars in their eyes and visions of government interference and control in America. They had been given a "dog and pony" show and bought it "hook, line, and sinker." One of the travelers, in referring to his trip to Russia, had the blindness to write, "I have seen the future, and it works."

The trends were aligned with these intellectuals in that age. It didn't take long for them, the people they supported, and the candidates they advanced to begin implementing more and more government control on the American public. The advance soldier in that process, unwittingly, was President Herbert Hoover. Confident of his own ability to take hold of the controls of government, he used the scare of the drop in the stock market of 1929 (which was not an emergency, did not shut down banks, and did not cause more suicides than New York had experienced even in the previous year; to explode just a few of the myths of that time) to begin meddling in industry and municipalities. A normal correction in an inflated exchange after a decade of real, substantial, economic growth (backed by actual expansion in GNP, GDP, and capital and productive capabilities, one of the largest growth decades in American history) was perfectly normal. The real question isn't what caused the temporary drop in aggregate stock values in October of 1929; the real question is why did the trouble persist so long after it happened? AND, why was there in fact a Depression within a Depression? (1933 and 1934 being worse than 1929 and 1930).

That brings us back to our "boatload of meddlers" and their trip to Russia. Men of their ilk were duped into believing all the emerging economic theories of their time; theories that all involved faulty economic assumptions and recommended more and more governmental interference in the money supply, markets, international trade, and spending. This meddling is what caused the runs on banks. This meddling is what took a small incident and prolonged it. This meddling is what stretched a short, normal, economic correction into an international catastrophe.

The actions of the following decades would usher in the "triumph of the welfare state" concept that still haunts us today. This is the idea that the government knows best, is responsible for fixing all problems, and can and should intermix itself in the affairs of economics and enterprise.

What happened in the late 20's and throughout the 30's is akin to a patient with a head cold getting advice from an over-reactive doctor. Based on some new, exciting techniques just picked up by the doctor at an international conference, the doctor administers drugs that don't treat the cold but make it worse. Seeing this, the good doctor, surrounded and encouraged by other doctors doing the same thing, confidently administers even more medicine. Only this time, there are additional side effects. The doctor, however, doesn't see it that way. Instead, he sees confirmation of just how sick this patient was in the first place and, gee whiz, good thing there's a doctor on the scene to help! Further meds produce more side effects and soon the situation is drastic. Emergency life support measures are required or else the patient will surely die. The patient is not really living any longer, strapped to the tubes and machines of life support as he is, but he is not dead either. This encourages the doctor and his colleagues to congratulate themselves on keeping such a terminal patient alive and strengthens their resolve to formalize the life support system. It is at this point that the doctors can't believe their ears when someone has the audacity to suggest that perhaps the patient never needed anything other than a chance to recover from his cold naturally. "As sick as he is?" they cry, "you non-doctors are so naive!"

This analogy is not meant to reflect poorly on doctors at all. It is directed at the intellectuals in government that operate under the false assumption that bureaucrats in Washington know better than our founding fathers, the forces of the free market that got us our prosperity in the first place, and the proven concept of representative government and individual freedom.

We have no need to take junkets to foreign countries looking for gold in their government strategies. We need to merely look to our own effective history. Groping around for new strategies and forming more and more government agencies is only killing the patient. We need fresh air. We need a little space to live naturally. We need freedom. Perhaps the intellectuals in Washington should hail a cab, take a trip to the Library of Congress, and read our founding documents. That would be a worthy junket!

William James is attributed to saying, "A great many people think they are thinking when they are merely rearranging their prejudices."

ROMANCE AND PERSISTENT CHEERINESS

One of my favorite authors is the late Patrick O'Brian. In an insightful description of one of his characters, he says that the person in question had made it to middle-age somehow without life "sanding the cheeriness" off of him. I loved that depiction. As with all art, it's beauty comes from its sublime alignment with reality.

You will find ample opportunity in your life to lose your cheeriness. Life is hard. There will be bad breaks and unfairness. Things will happen. Nobody promises smooth byways and easy streets, and if they do–run. But life is also wonderful. It is bright and interesting and full of the wonder of God's reflected glory. There is knowledge to gain, vast territories to explore, and ourselves to understand. There are extraordinary people of strength and heroic spirit. And there is the precious gift of time.

Romance, to me, is living life in full appreciation and awareness of the wonder of God's world. Romance means becoming, as Mark Twain said, "a prodigious noticer." Romance is finding pleasure in the small things; like the rippling sound of water against dock pilings, warm sun on skin, and the whisper of a toddler in your ear. Romance is noticing the sublime in big things; the danger and beauty of an ocean, the power and thrill of an airplane, the majesty and intimidation of a mountain. Romance is finding the good in others; their thoughtful gestures, their warm expressions of care, their smiles, their humor, and their friendship. Romance is shared experiences, memories, and inside jokes. Romance is designing your own home, taking care in your photography, expressing yourself through music or writing, and finishing a piece of wood. Romance can be the deposits of good into someone's life, giving a well-deserved but rare compliment, and buying a thoughtful gift.

189

Romance is the grateful expression of our ability, talent, warmth, and effort-just because. Romance is the steadiness of dependability, and the perseverance of the long-haul. Romance is family tradition and proud heritage. Romance is a choice.

Dissected or reduced to its component parts, romance disappears like a shy muse. Courted and summoned, romance sparkles and lights softly upon its caller. Clear thinking, pure motives, honest communications, and the service of others fuels the power of romance and appreciation in our lives. Selfishness, pressure, short-term thinking, and materialism wilt its wings and ruin its ability to please.

What I am talking about is the passionate expression of ourselves into our whole lives through the things we do, the people we touch, and the principles and the God for which we live. God has given us one life to live. It is given to each man once to die, and then the judgment. The world doesn't need any more dour Christians, but it doesn't need silly ignorance of our true condition, either. The world needs true joy that expresses itself in a spark in our eyes, suggesting that we have discovered the truth about life, ourselves, our Creator, and our purpose. It is then that they may call us romantics. May we take it as a compliment!

What personifies this concept in your life? What small things, or large, bring it into focus for you? At what moments do you feel the most "alive" and in touch with the cheeriness of your life? What gifts do you see around you in your life that remind you of your divine spark?

[W]hat counts is not necessarily the size of the dog in the f ight - it's the size of the fight in the dog. - Dwight Eisenhower

I have learned to use the word impossible with the greatest caution. - Wernher von Braun

The human spirit is stronger than anything that can happen to it. - C.C. Scott

SHARPEN THE SAW

Do you ever get run ragged? Ever grow weary in well doing? One of the key concepts author Stephen Covey talks about in *The Seven Habits of Highly Effective People* is that of sharpening the saw. Everybody needs to build a little time into their busy schedules to refresh and restore frayed nerve endings.

I travel a lot. And with travel comes friction. Flights are delayed or cancelled. Weather slows things down. Crowds are no fun. Hotels are expensive and have those noisy heater/air conditioner things that can keep you up all night. But one of the things travel makes me do is shut off the cell phone and read a good book. Sometimes, my flight time is the only time I can find for reading! And for me, reading is one of the best ways to stay sharp and restore myself.

Family time is also therapeutic. Exercise can be magical at bringing your spirits back to life. Certainly prayer and meditation should be primary, also. Sometimes just hanging out with some special people in your life can do the trick.

The key is to understand how you are wired and what you need to maintain yourself at peak performance. Do you know the leading indicators of frazzled nerve endings? Do you see signs of needing a break? Do you know what activities best restore you to top form? Be tuned in to these and book a little restoration time into your schedule.

There is a difference between being idle and resting, just as there is a difference between being busy and being effective. Idleness and busyness are two sides of the same coin: disorder. Their opposite is rest (read "rest-oration") and effectiveness, which come from an orderly life. Disciplined people have a way of both getting things done and resting once in a while. The two work together like a hand in a glove.

Winston Churchill painted landscapes. In the middle of political firestorms and a raging world war, he would sit serenely and paint for hours. Abraham Lincoln read humor books. In the midst of a calamitous civil war, he would entertain friends with chuckling short stories and witty jokes. Ronald Reagan would chop wood, ride horses, and clear trails. He was the leader of the free world and winning the Cold War, but he made time to swing an axe.

What are your methods of restoration? Do you schedule them effectively? If not, I'll bet you are busier than you need be, and less effective than you could be.

The test of a first-rate intelligence is the ability to hold two opposed ideas in the mind at the same time, and still retain the ability to function. One should, for example, be able to see that things are hopeless and yet be determined to make them otherwise. - F. Scott Fitzgerald

Too many people miss the silver lining because they're expecting gold. - Maurice Setter

We cannot direct the wind but we can adjust the sails. - Author Unknown

"The block of granite which was an obstacle in the pathway of the weak, became a stepping-stone in the pathway of the strong." - Thomas Carlyle

THE POWER OF
A TEAM

Learning leadership and people skills is necessary to function properly within a team. A team of people has tremendous power and potential if the participants are aligned in common purpose and dedicated to working toward the collective benefit of the group. Something wonderful happens as individuals strive together for common achievement and accomplishment: camaraderie.

As people work together, keeping their egos in check, working for the best ideas and holding back their own personal agendas while searching for an overall group agenda, momentum builds. The relationships between the team members strengthens, and the production, ideas, and *None of us is as good as all of us.* - Ray Kroc results are greater than the sum of the individual efforts. As McDonald's founder Ray Kroc said, "None of us is as good as all of us."

The challenge with many people is being able to work within a team. They lack the required people skills, confidence, or patience. They have to have their own way, or see their own idea advanced, and become a disruption to the healthy functioning of the team as their position predominates. After a while, they are either rejected from the team's activities, shunned, or the team becomes their personal dogmatic domain and fails to function anymore as a synergistic group. Another type of behavior destructive to teams is private conversations, gossip, or people too cowardly to address issues directly and publicly with the team or its members. Instead, they go around behind the scenes voicing their dissent and stirring up "discord among the brethren." Political factions develop, feelings are hurt, and unhealthy competition for power, position, or

193

prestige within the team develops. Again, under these conditions a team deteriorates and loses out on the powers of combined efforts.

I have been involved with both types of teams: those that function well and those that don't. The difference in the results between the two are not even in the same hemisphere. What made that difference was the people involved. Selfless, motivated, humble, energized, patient, caring people make the best teams. Often, unfortunately, one bad apple can ruin the whole mix. It only takes a little bit of arsenic to spoil a cake.

If you are fortunate enough to be involved in a team setting in some aspect of your life, strive to be the best teammate you can. Be a contributor, not a detractor. Deal open-handedly, not behind the scenes. Mean what you say and say what you mean. Listen, and appreciate the differences that others bring to the group. Be willing to change your opinion about something if presented with new information. A quote I recently heard said, "The world belongs to those who are willing to change their mind when presented with new facts." I can't tell you how many times I have gone into a team situation with a certain idea of what should be done or accomplished, but after hearing the great ideas and inputs of others, became convinced that my idea was not the best. Many times, I became convinced that my idea wasn't even any good! Sometimes my ideas have carried, but more often than not some amalgamation of everybody's ideas became the BEST idea. These situations are fun, energizing, and rewarding.

The world belongs to those who are willing to change their mind when presented with new facts.

Working as part of a team can be one of the best experiences people can have, or it can be among the worst. The only part of the experience you can control is your own contribution and behavior. Be a team player, and get ready for some rich experiences, and don't be surprised if at some point along the way you are called upon to take the lead!

THE UNIFORM OF LEADERSHIP IS THICK SKIN

Inspired by the statement, "When the going gets tough, the tough get going!"

Principles of Leadership Toughness:

1. It's not going to be fair (leaders often carry an unfair load)
2. Leadership is an inside job (nobody is responsible for motivating you, but yourself)
3. Expect obstacles and problems (remain calm, remember it's not what happens but how you respond, remember the axiom "This too shall pass," and stay committed to the purpose)
4. Success is never easy
5. "It's a long climb from the bottom and a short drop from the top" (don't get cocky, and don't stop doing what you did to get success in the first place)
6. Winners play hurt (remember the phrase "Doesn't matter, doesn't matter, doesn't matter . . . .)
7. It's always worth it to be a hero (you'll never regret the times you gave of yourself to others)
8. To be tough, you must find the source of your courage
9. Being tough does not include being mean, cold-hearted, bossy, or abusive.
10. The role of leadership requires the uniform of thick skin
11. Purpose is the key (you must be tough in the name of something. Find you purpose and live your life serving it)

Other points:

To make a difference, you've got to be different.

To make a stand, you've got to stand out.

You will be remembered for something, what will it be?

THE CHARACTER
TO BE A CHARACTER

There is a lot to be said for the concept of individuality. We have long celebrated the rugged individual, the loner, the stand-out, the rebel. There seems to be something attractive about a person who can remain what and who they are, even when under constant attack from "the world" and the court of "they" which are always on hand to apply pressure. Your parents told you to be one thing, your friends another, and now your college professors, boss, and co-workers give you more "guidance." It seems that these days, everyone from your closest friends to pundits in the media have an idea of who you should be.

The real question, however, is, "Do YOU know who you are? Do YOU know who you should be?"

For some reason there is a tendency for the masses to go along with the masses. Call it group think, the madness of crowds, or laziness.

Going along is the coward's way out, however. Standing firm for what one believes in, for who one is, and for those one loves is the essence of courage; it's the character to be a character!

Think about it: the most interesting characters in a novel are always those who are not afraid to be themselves, who are a little different, who stand apart as more authentic than the rest. We may marvel at their foibles, laugh at their idiosyncrasies, and maybe even judge them, but we always, deep down, admire them. I believe the reason for this is that, as Thoreau said, "Most men lead lives of quiet desperation." They are stuck inside a shell of a life that spends too much of its time seeking to please others and not enough following their calling; their true authentic purpose. But when we see someone with the character and courage to be their own person, lead by their own inner passion, following the calling given them by their Maker, we understand that we are witnessing greatness, and we long for it ourselves!

Incredibly, it is only a decision. A simple choice to become an individual, to think for yourself, to dare to be who you were created to be! As Charles Mackay wrote, "Men, it has been well said, think in herds; it will be seen that they go mad in herds, while they only recover their senses slowly, and one by one."

Misery is a communicable disease.
- Martha Graham

The world is full of cactus, but we don't have to sit on it.
- Will Foley

If you have the will to win, you have achieved half your success; if you don't, you have achieved half your failure.
- David Ambrose

A happy person is not a person in a certain set of circumstances, but rather a person with a certain set of attitudes.
- Hugh Downs

THE EXCELLENT MAN

I refer to author Jose Ortega y Gasset's classification of man into two distinct groups, the "mass man" (or "common man") vs. the "excellent man." As stated by Ortega,

". . . we distinguished the excellent man from the common man by saying that the former is the one who makes great demands on himself, and the latter the one who makes no demands on himself, but contents himself with what he is, and is delighted with himself. Contrary to what is usually thought, it is the man of excellence, and not the common man who lives in essential servitude. Life has no savor for him unless he makes it consist in service to something transcendental. Hence he does not look upon the necessity of serving as an oppression. This is life lived as a discipline - the noble life. Nobility is defined by the demands it makes on us - by obligations, not by rights. Noblesse oblige. 'To live as one likes is plebian; the noble man aspires to order and law' (Goethe)."

My favorite sentence in this paragraph is "Life has no savor for him unless he makes it consist in service to something transcendental." To me, that is the very definition of excellence; the service of something larger than ourselves, something significant, meaningful, and lasting. The "excellent" people are classified as such by choice, by the way they live their lives, and the purpose for which they strive. These people make demands upon themselves, they live a strenuous life in pursuit of greatness. Why? Because without such striving "life has no savor," in essence, life has no meaning, no joy, no fulfillment.

Here lies an interesting paradox; that the comfortable, easy life has an appealing appearance. However, for most of us, living a life of peace and affluence is unfulfilling and hollow. What appears alluring is actually fool's gold. Authentic satisfaction and happiness come when we sacrifice peace and affluence on the altar of significant service, accomplishment, and striving towards the desires of our hearts. It's when a man's actions are in line with the highest opinions and aspirations he holds for himself that he will feel the most alive. In fact, it is when he is the most alive.

Strive to be excellent. Make demands upon yourself to be all you can be. Serve others and live for a higher purpose. Read, study, and challenge yourself daily to improve. We mostly forget the hours of our lives spent in leisure, but those given in service to our calling will long be remembered by others.

Very often a change of self is needed more than a change of scene. - Arthur Christopher Benson

Some people are always grumbling because roses have thorns; I am thankful that thorns have roses. - Alphonse Karr

If you call a thing bad you do little, if you call a thing good you do much." - Johann Wolfgang von Goethe

THERE IS NO READY

"The song that I came to sing remains unsung to this day.
I have spent my days in stringing and in unstringing my
instrument.
The time has not come true, the words have not been rightly set;
Only there is the agony of wishing in my heart."
- Rabindranath Tagore

How many people never stop to consider that they came to sing a song? Of those few who are aware of it, how many of them waste their days "stringing and unstringing" their instrument?

People are experts at getting ready for things; getting ready for college, getting ready for the wedding, getting ready for their first home, getting ready for vacation, getting ready for football season, getting ready for the holidays, getting ready to hit their goals, getting ready to build their business, getting ready to go on that diet, getting ready to get ready to live, once and only once they are ready.

But we will never be "ready."

There is no "ready."

There are only days of our lives.

"Ready" is the devil's trick to steal from us the wonder of God's gift of time.

You were born a magnificent creation to begin with.

So stop getting ready.

Play the song you were born to play.

Now.

LEADERSHIP HUNGER

The core of becoming a leader is hunger. This could be hunger for success, hunger for significance, hunger for change, hunger for the rescue of people in harm's way. Whatever the nature of the hunger, and there are certainly healthy and unhealthy hungers, hunger is the foundational spark that leads to the influence of others.

It is interesting to me as I observe people growing in leadership that it is always true that their ability to gain influence and have an affect on the conditions around them is always proportional to their passion for the vision. A leader simply cannot stand to leave things as he or she found them. There is a burning feeling that something must be done, accomplished or achieved, and set aright.

It is my personal belief that the proper sources of hunger are God-given. As an interesting point of reflection, author Ravi Zachariasis recently wrote that "Christ's salvation transforms a person's hungers." This is extremely interesting to contemplate and understand. Many leaders are perhaps driven by unhealthy hungers: the desire to be pre-eminent, the desire for fame, the desire for wealth and comfort and self-aggrandizement. This hunger can actually lead to good things, as the leader achieves and accomplishes. But this type of hunger is short-lived and can only lead to emptiness in the least and destruction in the greatest. Legitimate, God-given hunger produces a drive that transcends pride of person and establishes itself as a monument to God's grace. It produces good fruit in the lives of others and fulfills the God-following

We should all fight to find our God-given calling, and then stoke the flames of the hunger of that vision as hard as we can.

leader. This is the type of hunger I speak of when I refer to the hunger of a leader.

We should all fight to find our God-given calling, and then stoke the flames of the hunger of that vision as hard as we can. We should feel driven by that inner desire to do what God built us to do while we still have the time. Our days are numbered, but we have been given enough to accomplish what God will lead us to do for his kingdom and glory, in his infinite wisdom and plan.

Don't waste your life in a comfortable passage of the time you've been given. Don't set yourself up for that chief regret of looking backward over a life filled with blessings but devoid of service to a cause greater than yourself. Find your purpose and calling, and plug in to the true source of healthy hunger. Give yourself to that cause, and do all to the glory of God. As one of my favorite verses states, "Let your light so shine that others will see your good works and glorify your Father which is in heaven." (Matthew 5:16)

SOFTNESS AND SOCIALISM

It is impossible to truly read history without weeping. Tales of suffering, injustice, violence and loss are staggeringly pervasive across the whole sweep of human history. It matters little whether one consults the Middle Ages, the Age of Rome, the Classical period, or our own modern era; proof of fallen human nature abounds. People are murdered for their color or religion, or simply because they are in the wrong territory, or many times just because they are weaker. Women are raped and sold into prostitution, children hauled away as slaves. Disease, famine, malnourishment, hunger and thirst are everywhere throughout history.

I could get even more graphic describing Roman crucifixions, dark ages torture, the Rape of Manchuria, the Holocaust, or the genocide carried out by the communists. The list is literally endless.

Contrast this bleak portrait with our society today. We have every accommodation and luxury from good and plentiful food to effective and accessible medicines to air conditioning and refrigeration. In North America, at least, we still have the Rule of Law and some protection for the sanctity of the individual (aborted babies not included). In short, we live in peace, comfort, and ease.

This modern living has produced a population of people who are soft and spoiled, unaccustomed to struggle or suffering and quick to whine and complain if their coffee is too hot or a flight is delayed by weather. Luxury and peace, comfort and accommodation have bred a people devoid of grit and toughness.

There is another weakening agent that has crept into our society: socialistic thinking. Unfortunately this has become most prevalent among young people. After years of "social indoctrination" in our public schools, we now have a growing voting public who do not believe in absolute truth, the Rule of Law, or the sanctity of the individual. Instead they hail the power of government, the "right" of entitlement, and the failed promises of egalitarianism.

If you combine these two elements, softness and socialism, even for a while into a society, you are playing with fire. Great civilizations rarely fall from enemies external; they almost always crumble from within.

As the "Greatest Generation," those from World War II who were toughened during the Great Depression and proved their mettle fighting for freedom during the second world war, passes away (over 1000 are reported to be dying each day), I fear our country is losing the fabric of greatness which built it and brought it through many storms. As those heroes die, young people are growing up to replace them. What will be their legacy? Are those of us in our prime now doing all we can to emulate the Greatest Generation by refusing to fall for the complacency offered by our comforts? Are we educating ourselves and others about the false preachings of socialistic ideas and policies?

If we don't, who will? Who will set the example of toughness, showing the generations to follow that it is okay to struggle and work hard, to sacrifice and strive mightily? Who will sound the warning bell that socialistic and entitlement thinking are false religions that always lead to destruction? If we don't, make no mistake: history WILL repeat itself. And what does history offer to those who ignore its lessons? Pain and suffering.

WE CREATED THEM

"The significant problems we face cannot be solved at the same level of thinking we were at when we created them."
- Albert Einstein

Success requires proper thinking. Notice in this famous quote how Einstein, without stopping to defend his supposition, as if it were just the most obvious thing in the world, basically says that our thinking created our significant problems.

Our *thinking*?

If you listen to many of the political pundits these days you would not be lead to believe that our thinking created our significant problems. Rather you would learn that our parents are to blame, or the our ancestors, or the color of our skin, or our socio-economic standing, or American imperialism, or an unfair educational system, or tax breaks for the rich, or . . . all of these reasons and more are sold to the American public as the reason for the significant problems we face. It follows naturally, then, if the problems are not your fault, they must be somebody else's. This would then extend to mean that someone else is responsible for fixing them! Oh, how *the people* love this kind of stuff! Anyone who comes along and blames their problems on others, relieves them of personal responsibility for fixing them, and promises easy solutions "if you vote for me" has a ready-made following.

Unpopular, however, is the person that dares to suggest that people are the creator of their own problems. First, that would require getting people to admit responsibility - always a dangerous thing. Second, it would imply that the person himself would be responsible for fixing his problems - shear heresy! Third, it would feel harsh and unfair, and you know how sensible our feelings are these days.

Am I being tongue-in-cheek? Do you think so? Sadly, I think not.

Step One in success thinking is realizing that we are responsible. We might not be entirely to blame, but that is beside the point. Blame never accomplishes anything. We, and we alone, are responsible for our conduct and our results. Any time we try to assign that responsibility to others we lose freedom on the altar of negligence. As we allow someone else power over our results, we give them proportional power over our conduct. It can work no other way.

Step Two is realizing that thinking is what produces problems or gains. Our actions flow from our thinking, and our results flow from our actions. Our thinking is what is responsible.

So how do we take control of our lives and utilize our freedom? By learning to think properly about success, personal responsibility, and the results we have in our lives. By confronting brutal reality as it actually is, then owning up to the steps we can take to make an impact on that reality. The way out of our problems is neither blaming others nor asking for their help in digging out, but rather learning to think better than we did when we made our messes originally, then changing behavior accordingly. It is difficult, but it is the only way out of an endless cycle. As the saying goes, "If you want to change some things in your life, you've got to change some things in your life." Try starting with your thinking.

Just think about it.

I never really look for anything. What God throws my way comes. I wake up in the morning and whichever way God turns my feet, I go. - Pearl Bailey

Men who never get carried away should be. - Malcolm Forbes

Become a possibilitarian. No matter how dark things seem to be or actually are, raise your sights and see possibilities - always see them, for they're always there. - Norman Vincent Peale

KEY QUESTIONS

The only bad experience is the unevaluated experience. Although experience gives the test first and the lesson later, it would be even more tragic to have the experience and never bother to get the lesson!

The best way to evaluate our experiences, and thereby make the most of them, is to ask proper questions. Here are a few to get your brain working:

1. What one thing could I change (or do), that would make an enormous difference/improvement in what I am doing? Why am I not already doing it?
2. What mistake am I currently making that I may not even know about?
3. What is my biggest blind spot?
4. What is the biggest thing I have learned about myself recently?
5. What is the number one thing I am trying to change about myself right now?

That's enough for now. Too many questions loses the focus. This should be enough to get you started. Ask these types of questions of yourself on a regular basis and grow more from your experiences.

Surrounded by people who love life, you love it too; surrounded by people who don't, you don't. - Mignon McLaughlin

Physical strength is measured by what we can carry; spiritual by what we can bear. - Author Unknown

MENTORING: LEARNING TO THINK THROUGH LIFE

I read a fantastic article by Rick Beneteau on giving and listening. It reminded me of the role of mentoring in helping someone think properly through their life. Life can be tough and it certainly isn't always a bed of roses. If life is tough for everyone, why do some people seem to ride the waves from peak to peak, but others are buried by the waves? I believe it is not what happens to you in life, but how you think about what happens to you in life that matters most. Do you see your current challenges, roadblocks, and setbacks as evidence of no opportunity or do you see the same situations as evidence that God has a BIG plan for you? Think about it for a minute! If God is calling you for a big assignment, wouldn't it make sense that He would place some major challenges in your life to develop character first? God must develop the person for the assignment given and challenges are a great way to develop the necessary character for advanced assignments. Instead of fighting our fate, let's be drawn to our destiny.

It is not what happens to you in life, but how you think about what happens to you in life that matters most.

When my wife Laurie and I sit down to mentor couples, we tell them to share with us the good, the bad, and the ugly. We are not listening so we can have a pity party with the couple. We listen to celebrate the good, make adjustments for the bad and address the ugly immediately. Every great leader has had good, bad and ugly things happen to them, but the key is how they are thinking through the situations. How are you thinking through the good, the bad, and the ugly in your life? Do you secretly enjoy the bad and the ugly things that are happening? Many people surprisingly

209

do! The reason for this secret enjoyment is they feel it justifies their lack of results and causes others to feel sorry for them. DO NOT EVER PLAY THE ROLE OF VICTIM! It may feel good to have others feel sorry for you, but it is a drug that creates a harmful life addiction. YOU are a champion and all champions will have to overcome the bad and the ugly in their life.

We are not training people to be victims, so take the bad things that happen to you as God's way of developing character. The greatest gift a mentor can give to you is the absolute belief that you have what it takes inside of you to overcome your present difficulties and win in the game of life. Laurie and I believe strongly that all of us have what it takes and we have dedicated our life to teach others how to think through their difficulties to be champions in the game of life! We must give to others, but the best thing to give to others is a champion's way of thinking through life. Anything else that we give to them is giving less than our personal best.

LEADERSHIP FEEDBACK

Let's talk briefly about the topic of leadership feedback. I believe it is of the utmost importance that you listen to the feedback from those you lead. Without feedback, you run the risk of leading people into irrelevancy. I may not like feedback, but I don't like irrelevancy at all. It is important for the leaders to get the truth from the troops so they can make accurate decisions based upon the facts. So many leaders cocoon themselves around "yes men" and straighten deck chairs while the *Titanic* sinks.

It is important for the leaders to get the truth from the troops so they can make accurate decisions based upon the facts.

What type of leader are you? Do you act like you have all the answers or are you humble enough to seek feedback? The leaders of today must know that no one person can have all the answers and only a team will win big.

MORE GOVERNMENT = WRONG ANSWER

The Great Depression is the classic example of what happens to a free market economy when government geniuses think they can make better decisions than millions of free consumers. What started out as a normal market correction was followed by government interference in the form of price fixing, output caps, increased taxes, rampant government spending, huge protective tariffs, and government meddling in areas that should have been left to free enterprise (power and lighting, among others), which effectively prolonged a recession, spawned a depression, then created an even bigger "depressions within a depression."

Franklin Delano Roosevelt (FDR) (Democrat) became famous for his "fireside chats." His smooth voice and fatherly reassurances calmed a nation on the front end while he yanked and pulled on every string available to government on the back end. The President that preceded him, Hebert Hoover (Republican), was no better. Between their two administrations, the U.S. government began to meddle in American affairs more so than at any other time since the Civil War.

At first, the government experimented with different manipulations, looking for the right combination to "fix" things, all the while being sure to appear as if they were "doing" things on behalf of Americans. Then, they began prosecuting all kinds of scapegoats to take the American people's minds off the fact that all of the changes weren't working and to place the blame elsewhere. This persecution was against former Treasury secretaries in the previous administrations, small business owners who were accused of violating some brand new, super-complicated tax rule, large industries that were operating exactly how they always had but somehow were suddenly being called illegal, and stock traders and investors. The sensational news stories about the government cracking down on the people that had "caused all of this" kept their minds distracted from the real culprits. It was an era in American history that mirrored Caesar's "bread and circuses" program in which he pacified and distracted the mobs in Rome with free grain and gladiatorial games.

Let me be as clear as I can be: more government is not the answer. It never has been, and never will be.

It has been tried.

It has failed.

Every time.

Why must we repeat it again?

Why must we dive into the same terrible spiral of suffering and blame and flagging economics and loss of freedoms and encroaching bureaucracies, only to discover that they still don't work?

FDR called his escapade of government manipulation the "New Deal." It is safe to say that much of the New Deal was an extremely raw deal. Now we are entering into an era where people seem to count more and more on the government for "answers" and "fixes" to problems that it created in the first place! Only what do you call it after the New Deal is found not to work? Do you call it an Even Newer Deal? Or the This-Time-It-Will-Be-Better New Deal?

Let's keep it simple folks: More government = Wrong Answer!

They that can give up essential liberty to obtain a little temporary safety deserve neither liberty nor safety.
- Benjamin Franklin

We have enjoyed so much freedom for so long that we are perhaps in danger of forgetting how much blood it cost to establish the Bill of Rights. - Felix Frankfurter

"No man can put a chain about the ankle of his fellow man without at last finding the other end fastened about his own neck." - Frederick Douglass

LAUNCHING AN ARMADA: BUYER BEWARE

Philip II of Spain's father was a brilliant soldier and states-man named Charles V, and when he passed on, he left the world's largest empire in the hands of his son. Philip had been trained since childhood in the arts of leadership and diplomacy. At age sixteen he was made Regent of Spain. His "marriage of conquest" was to the Queen of England, Mary Tudor (known to history as "Bloody Mary" for her butchery of Protestants). Philip was handed the world's largest empire, encompassing the largest territory, the most colonies, the best ports, and access to more natural resources than any other country. But during his long reign, he would manage to squander away his position atop the world's heap of power, and through his mistakes, allow a fledgling little island country led by an indecisive Queen to plant the seeds that would grow into world dominance.

What happened? You might not be surprised to learn that it came down to leadership.

A quasi-war of sorts had been waged between England and Spain for decades. Queen Elizabeth's "gentleman pirates," including Francis Drake, John Hawkins, Walter Raleigh, Martin Frobisher, and Charles Howard, had pecked and picked away at Spain's holdings in the New World, and had managed to disrupt and even steal large amounts of South American treasure bound for Spain's coffers. Drake's circumnavigation of the globe and capture of one of Spain's largest treasure galleons was only one example of the daring feats the English carried out at Spain's expense. In the meantime, King Philip was behind numerous assassination attempts directly aimed at Queen Elizabeth, and the two countries were at war against each other for the religious choice of the people of the Netherlands.

When Queen Elizabeth sentenced Mary, Queen of Scots, to death for treason (a confirmed assassination attempt on Elizabeth), it brought the two countries to the edge of declared war. Philip began preparations to amass a large armada of ships that would sail in something called The Enterprise of England. The "Enterprise" was supposed to be a secret plan to attack the island of England itself, but the large-scale buildup of supplies and ships in Spain's ports could hardly go unnoticed. Sir Francis Drake was able to delay the launch of the Armada by at least a year by attacking and destroying a major fleet of ships and supplies in the port of Cadiz.

Then, somehow, peace negotiations were proffered. Diplomats from both sides began testing the waters for terms of settlement. Queen Elizabeth, despite violent opposition from nearly every one of her advisors, was extremely interested in a peaceful settlement. England was a small island country, by no means able to match the enormous wealth and stature of Spain, and it had virtually no way to defend itself should armed forces actually land on her shores. Queen Elizabeth was also a bit of a realist, and she understood the enormous cost of fighting the world's only Super Power in a protracted war. For these reasons, she was able to make huge concessions for the peace process as long as they didn't compromise her principles and the things she had promised her people.

King Philip, however, was not disposed towards peace. He sat atop the World's richest empire, its largest military, he held most of Europe under his control, he had recently annexed Portugal and with it enormous territory in the East Indies to add to his dominance in the West Indies. According to author Neil Hanson, "Philip's correspondence shows that he gave not the slightest thought to any compromise. He could have had peace in the Netherlands on several occasions, but [as Philip said himself], 'With regard to Holland and Zealand or any other province or towns, the first step must be for them to receive and maintain alone the exercises of the Catholic religion and to subject themselves to the Roman church, without tolerating the exercise of any other religion . . . There is to be no flaw, no change, no concession by convention or otherwise of liberty of conscience or religious peace, or anything of that sort.'"

Although Elizabeth was all for the concession of allowing religious tolerance, Philip was dead against any "liberty of conscience" whatsoever. It became a classic struggle of tyranny versus freedom of choice, of big versus small, Goliath pushing around David. Again, according to Hanson, "[the entire conflict] was partly about money . . . partly about political and dynastic imperatives, and partly about the loss of face that Philip had suffered through attacks on his own coast, but it was also genuinely driven by religious fundamentalism and Philip's obsession with restoration of Europe to the Catholic faith. A flexible and pragmatic ruler in his youth, he was now a stubborn and dogmatic old man, brooding alone . . . . the only solution that would satisfy him would be the overthrow of Elizabeth and the total destruction of the Dutch rebellion."

Instead of negotiating for peace in good faith, Philip played games. In his own words: "I declare that my intention is that these negotiations shall never lead to any result, whatever conditions the English may offer. On the contrary, the only object is to deceive them and to cool them in their preparations for defense, by making them believe such preparations will not be necessary."

Analyzing the details of this history, we see that Philip's fatal choice to launch the Armada against England came from the following four factors:

1. Money
2. Political and dynastic imperatives (nepotism and power)
3. The loss of face (pride)
4. Religious fundamentalism (tyranny and the suppression of freedom)

The details of the Armada, its mammoth size, its incredible expense to Spain's treasury, and its resulting failure, are story enough for a future book. But the launching and failure of the Spanish Armada in 1588 represented the "high water mark" in the world-dominance of Spain. Its cost, and its loss of prestige for Spain throughout the world, were blows too large from which to recover. Even though Philip had inherited the world's largest power from his father, he would hand it on as a much reduced, debt-ridden, and shrinking power. England, a tiny island country, would rise on the ashes of the fading Spain and over the course of time would rise to become the world's largest empire, and it would hold that position for a long time until one of its former colonies, The United States of America, would gain that position in the twentieth century. The entire period from the Armada in the sixteenth century to the beginning of World War I, with the American Revolution as the sole exception, would witness the rise and dominance of Great Britain as the world's pre-eminent empire.

Leadership is critical to the success of any endeavor. Leaders lead best when motivated by visions that build up instead of destroy, that seek to help rather than hinder, and that become more concerned about what can be accomplished than by who can be oppressed. In the case of Philip II of Spain, his motivations were all wrong. Money, power, pride, and oppression of the freedoms of others became the seeds of his own destruction. At many points along the way he could have made an acceptable peace with a smaller, but stubbornly principled and belligerent nation - but he would have nothing of it. It was all or nothing for Philip. He made his choice accordingly, and his empire dwindled to insignificance as a result.

Remember the story of the Armada as you lead in your life. Be careful of your motivations. Never get suckered into believing that oppressing the freedoms of others, grabbing for money, fighting for power, or struggling to regain lost pride are worthy pursuits. Don't get fooled into launching your own "Enterprise of England." If you do, you can rely on having to face a Sir Francis Drake, a Sir Walter Raleigh, or any number of individual privateers who will take to the waters to oppose you. And never underestimate the power of a storm or two to dash your ships on the rocky shores.

It's much better to lead from a position of integrity, to fight for good, to stand for freedom, and to defend the individual and his or her rights. That's the side on which all the heroes of history have found themselves. That's the side on which the true leaders live!

Lead on, and if you lead for good, fear no Armada that comes against you!

THE TEMPTATION OF REMOVING HUMAN FREEDOM

One thing that is a common temptation for leaders is to lose patience with higher-level forms of influence and instead resort to an authoritarian style. After all, isn't it easier to bark out orders and make demands, flexing one's authority muscles and showing subordinates your stripes? I ran across a great paragraph by author Dan B. Allender in his excellent book *Leading with a Limp:*

> "The temptation for all leaders is to encroach on human freedom and take away the suffering of humanity through some form of authoritarian order. Indulging this temptation underlies the fascism of all utopias. Removing human freedom is done with sincerity and the desire to serve the forsaken and bent brood of humanity. But all of this is a lie. If limiting human freedom tempted Jesus before he began his calling as the Christ, then it will conceivable be an ongoing temptation for all who fall into leadership."

First, one can clearly see where compassionate politicians take a wrong turn. With misplaced compassion, they propose programs and government agendas to relieve the sufferings and hardships of certain peoples, only to end up limiting human freedoms in the process. And it is a short argument to state that government is better at messing things up than they are at executing programs. It is almost a rule that government programs grow and take on an unmanageable growth-life of their own. What may begin sincerely enough as a measure to help others (giving the benefit of the doubt and ignoring the very likely possibility that there is self-serving "vote selling" involved, as well), apparently well-meaning politicians end up actually limiting human freedoms and accomplishing the opposite of what they claim they intended. As Ronald Reagan said, "The scariest words you could ever hear are; I'm from the Government and I'm here to help."

So much for politicians. What about companies? It seems there is always controversy swirling regarding some form of competition among companies: those that cry unfair competition with others, those that want government protection against foreign competition, those that try to monopolize their position in the marketplace instead of having to face the pressures of competition. But all of business life is about competition. Competition is the gymnasium of discomfort from which stronger companies emerge. The history of business in free enterprise societies shows that the society, through its customers, is nearly always better served when competition is allowed to reign freely. Any time it is constrained artificially, or when certain entities are given a pass from the rigors of competition, the customers and society suffer. Examples are plenty, such as the de-regulation of the phone companies and the airline industry. Another is the market-driven de-regulation of the software industry through the concept of open source programs. Each of these shake-ups spawned new days of freedom in those industries, and while change was painful and even fatal for some of the more entrenched and inflexible entities, the result was lower prices and better service for customers, and an improved competitive environment for companies that not only made the surviving ones better, but became a breeding ground for a host of new, agile, creative players on the scene.

One of my favorite examples of this is Southwest airlines, which had a competitive new idea and such excellent execution of its idea that the old, stodgy, poor-service, entrenched airlines didn't want to have to compete with the new upstart. Instead, the "big boys" resorted to lawsuits. They determined to utilize the full strength of their corporate financial resources to protect their territory. Their strategy was that it would be easier to litigate a competitor to death rather than to beat them on the open field of play. Kill them while they were young, so to speak. After over a decade, however, Southwest airlines prevailed. Southwest Airlines not only survived the legal decimation strategy of scared-to-compete competitors, but have become a "big boy" themselves, consistently remaining the most profitable airline on the continent.

So much for companies. What of individuals? This is where we really want to focus. In our experience with leaders the authoritarian style always appears to be the amateur approach. This is because, as Dan Allender so aptly points out, it is the easiest and most automatic. Without thinking, someone in a position of authority (and this can even be observed among little children) most easily sinks to a level of relying upon position for influence. John Maxwell calls this Positional Leadership. It is the lowest level of influence. "Do this because I have authority over you." And sometimes, the reason given by the leader for such behavior is the level of chaos encountered and the need for drastic action. Certainly, there is a time for this, but it is rare. More often, influence of a higher order is called for. I find it interesting that Allender calls this tendency for leaders to slip into authoritarian influence a temptation. If he is correct, we as leaders should always be on guard against our tendencies for control, and work ever harder to adhere to our purposes of influence and cause.

The Five Levels of Influence we discuss in the *Launching a Leadership Revolution* book are to serve as a roadmap away from this temptation toward authoritarian leadership. Corporations, small businesses, governments, homes, churches, and community organizations will all be better served by leaders that understand the nature of true influence.

Real leaders have influence because people want to follow them.

Real leaders have influence because people want to follow them.

Real leaders have influence because others buy into them.

Real leaders have influence because people get caught up in their vision.

Real leaders have influence because others buy into their cause.

Real leaders have influence because they have character, get results, share the credit, and accept the blame.

I wonder how much better our society would be if our politicians, corporate leaders, and individual leaders at every level of society understood these basic truths?

LEAVE A LEGACY

It was another dreary winter day and after 10 hours of walking the factory floor my body was exhausted. There had to be more to life than just working to pay the bills. My mind drifted back to my youth and all the crazy dreams I had as a child. I was going to be someone and believed I would succeed. I chuckled at my youthful fantasies and thought how naïve I had been, but inside was the small voice that whispered to me of my destiny. It whispered of a legacy that I was leaving unfulfilled. It's not like I hated my life, but it just wasn't a life that was making a difference. Yes, the fuel pumps I worked on as an engineer were quieter than the model before and yes I did receive four patents and a national benchmarking award for the design, but would anyone claim the sound of their fuel pump was the difference maker in their life? If significance was possible, why not strive for it? I would have to work hard whether I achieved great things or not, so why not shoot for leaving a legacy? My mind argued with itself, "Legacy? Legacies are for Washington's, Franklin's, Lincolns, Edison's, Ford's, and the like. But didn't they start out as just kids with a dream just like me? Wasn't it possible for a kid growing up in Columbiaville, Michigan to achieve just as much as anyone else? Maybe I would achieve more if I just set bigger goals for life?" Getting into my car, I vowed that I would pursue my dreams no matter what. That I would endure any criticism, fight any battle and surmount any obstacle to live a life of meaning and significance. Legacies are not handed out at birth; they are crafted through dreams, goals, personal development, courage and

Legacies are not handed out at birth; they are crafted through dreams, goals, personal development, courage and commitment.

commitment. Anyone can claim a spot among the legends of American heroes if they are willing to dream, believe, and work towards their legacy, regardless of the criticism and setbacks. A legacy is a gift given back to your family name and something that future generations of your family will look to in times of hardship. Imagine if you were a descendant of George Washington and were going through struggles. You could look back to President Washington's life and realize that he surmounted many struggles on his journey of leaving a legacy also. If we are going to live a life, then might as well make it a life that counts.

As a child growing up I always had to work hard in sports to make up for my lack of size. As a freshman I weighed 98 pounds soaking wet and stood a massive 5 feet tall. Why I went out for the basketball team is a good question, but I believed I could work hard and achieve. Many of life's greatest lessons are learned in losses and we endured a winless season with many embarrassing losses. I had my share of losing, enough to last a lifetime, but life continued to give me more than my fair share. The next debacle was my attempt at playing baseball as a sophomore. I played "left out" and deserved the position. It wasn't until my junior year that I started playing the sports that suited my abilities. In cross country, wrestling, and track it wasn't size that counted as much as heart. I learned that hard work, basic training, and focus can produce better results than dabbling a little in everything. I would go home after a successful day of running and tell my mom and dad about the race. Many times my dad would share about his races when he ran cross country. Some times he would talk about his dad and how he was a top track star and this would feed my faith that I could achieve more. I loved when my dad would tell the Woodward children about the history of the family. What a loss that more families do not instill the pride of their family name to their children. I grew up learning about my great-great-grandfather who pulled himself out of poverty and owned a hotel and restaurants through hard work and big dreams. I learned about Woodward's who owned hotels in Florida and how the Woodward's once had been successful and owned many properties. Dad would then regretfully add that the prodigal spending habits had made the Woodward's a lower-middle-class family again. These stories fueled my dream to return the Woodward family to its former stature. What is your family's history? Have you ever thought about your family's legacy to date and what part you will play in this legacy?

Each individual family member has a choice of what to do with their family's legacy. Some may say, "My family does not have a legacy. No one has ever achieved anything of significance in my family." My answer is if that is true then you will be the first to strive for greatness. Be a script changer for your family. Every legendary family started with no legacy, but with a man or woman with a dream in their heart. Others may say, "My family is already very successful and I have nothing to add." My answer is to be a script completer and continue your family legacy. You have greatness inside of you and your family has already displayed the way. Maybe your family legacy is an embarrassment to you, but this should be looked as a challenge to change your family's legacy. Each generation that is born has a responsibility to establish, change or continue their family legacy. Many choose to ignore their responsibilities of their family name and never attempt anything great to enhance it. I believe that every family has greatness inside of them and for many it is just a question of changing their limiting beliefs. As individuals have limiting beliefs, so do families. I tell my children, "when the going gets tough, just remember that you are a Woodward and you will find a way to endure and win." We must help generate the winning beliefs in our families that will help them overcome the obstacles on their own way to their legacies.

We must help generate the winning beliefs in our families that will help them overcome the obstacles on their own way to their legacies.

All of this has been said to get to this question, "What family legacy will you leave to posterity?" If you are like many then you have never asked this question before. This is alright, because we are asking it now and it is never too late. As you realize that your life is part of the chain that links the past to the future though the present, then you will understand your responsibility to make your life count. Every successful leader develops his legacy through:

1. Character
2. Relationships
3. Task

Character

Laurie and I have been blessed with great parents, mentors and friends who are constantly encouraging us in our endeavors, but it wasn't always this way. When Laurie and I first started to dream big, our families thought we were crazy. We heard so many negative comments that we almost believed it and gave up. This is where character comes in. If you are going to achieve anything worthwhile you must sell yourself first. After you are sold yourself, remember that being true to yourself is the beginning of character. When a person makes a decision to move ahead in life, they must also expect obstacles to test their character and resolve. No one achieves greatness without strength of character and I am encouraging you to work on this first. Without character the other two do not matter.

Relationships

Relationships help you to develop your legacy, because no one achieves lasting success by themselves. No one is truly a self-made person. Laurie and I have been blessed with some incredible friends and mentors. These are people who will give you perspective when you are struggling, encouragement when needed, and cheers during your victories. Cultivate friendships through being a friend. Jesus said, "It is more blessed to give than receive." What if everyone lived by this motto? Can you imagine a world where everyone attempted to out-serve one another? I know this is idealistic, but I would rather be an idealist and be let down once in a while than be a pessimist and be right all the time. The people who have achieved the most have achieved through helping others achieve their best. Be a servant to others and you will be amazed at the harvest you reap from sowing into other's lives. This will greatly enhance your legacy, because your greatest legacy will be in the lives in which you made a difference. If I asked you to name the last five Super Bowl winners, the last five World Series winners, and the last five NBA champions, you would likely struggle to get them right, but if I asked you to name five people who have made a difference in your life, you would have no problem. Why is that? Even though the teams listed are champions, they made no impact on your personal life. A leader makes a personal impact, and this makes all the difference.

Task

Task is the last factor in building a legacy. You can have character, have strong relationships, but you must also press towards the goal. This involves setting goals and accomplishing tasks. The key here is to never accomplish tasks and blow the relationship. Remember your true legacy is in teaching others how to accomplish in life and this is impossible if you offend them in the lessons. A leader constantly asks how he can accomplish his task through teaching others. The more that is accomplished without one person doing it all, the more someone is leveraging character and relationships to achieve a specific task. One of the greatest joys of a legacy builder is for them to help a team accomplish a task and give all the credit to the team. A leader is less interested in recognition for himself and more interested in recognition for his team. We will accomplish much more with a large team ego and not a large personal ego. Legacies are achieved through leadership which is accomplished through the development of character, relationships and tasks.

Legacies are achieved through leadership which is accomplished through the development of character, relationships and tasks.

Many will tell me, "But I don't think I have what it takes to be a great leader." I am living proof that everything it takes to lead is already inside of you and it is your responsibility to develop the hunger and bring it out. No one would have accused me of being a leader in high school. I had no concept of what it meant to positively influence anyone. To learn leadership, start a program of personal development. Begin to read life-enhancing books, listen to leaders on CD, and associate with as many leaders as possible. The old saying, "If you hang out with dogs you get fleas" is so true. Hang out with leaders and capture the vision of your family legacy. I dare you to attempt something great! I dare you as you walk out of work tomorrow to dream bigger! I stopped waiting for my ship to come in and decided to build my own.

One of my favorite quotes is, "When all is said and done, much more is said than is ever done." Don't be remembered as someone who talked a great game, but never played.

FINISHING WELL

There is an abundance of sayings that address the concept of beginning something. "A journey of a thousand miles begins with the first step," and "starting is more than half of finishing," are just two that come immediately to mind. But it seems to me that finishing is more important than starting.

Let me explain. In my lifetime, I've seen a lot of people start things; projects, businesses, jobs, careers, relationships, whatever. And I've done a lot of starting myself. But I have noticed that there are way more things begun than finished. As a matter of fact, I have come to think that the art of finishing is what separates the truly great leaders from the rest.

Finishing well is a concept that begs consideration. Many leaders begin the journey, but only few finish. And even fewer finish well.

J. Robert Clinton and Richard W. Clinton wrote that there are seven main barriers to finishing well:

1. Finances - their use and abuse
2. Power - its abuse
3. Inordinate pride - which leads to downfall
4. Sex - illicit relationships
5. Family - critical issues
6. Plateauing
7. Emotional and Psychological Wounding

A quick review of this list will have every leader's head nodding as he or she realizes they have either been sidetracked or tempted by one or many of these, or have known someone who has fallen to one of these culprits. But I found most helpful the list of things leaders can do to enhance their chances of finishing well, as given to those authors by their mentor, whom they refer to only as "Pastor Ray:"

1. Gain and keep a broad perspective
2. Develop an expectancy for renewal
3. Practice disciplines, especially spiritual ones
4. Develop and maintain a learning posture
5. Have and listen to mentors

(paraphrased, taken from *Leaders on Leadership*, edited by George Barna).

As leaders on the journey to significance, I think it would benefit each of us to take these five enhancements to heart. Remember:

Any one can start,
and many do.
Few finish well,
it's up to you.

We all live under the same sky, but we don't all have the same horizon. - Konrad Adenauer

We can destroy ourselves by cynicism and disillusion, just as effectively as by bombs. - Kenneth Clark

The impossible can always be broken down into possibilities. - Author Unknown

An adventure is only an inconvenience rightly considered. An inconvenience is only an adventure wrongly considered. - G.K. Chesterton

Impossible is a word only to be found in the dictionary of fools. - Napoleon

FREEDOM UNDER FIRE - FROM REPUBLIC TO EMPIRE TO ?

In the United States we are proud of our freedom. We salute our flag to honor those who have sacrificed to win it for us. We say a pledge to a flag which stands for the ideals upon which our nation was founded. We teach our children that they live in a free country and can grow up to do whatever they want.

Sure, ours is not a perfect country. Its founding ideals have never quite been matched by its behavior. In its early history this was most obviously marked by slavery, followed by genocide of the continent's natives, and discrimination that persists in some forms even to this day.

While these stories are old and well-known, the new atrocities committed by our country are in the same category: the infringement of people's freedoms. Just as slavery and the wiping out of native Americans was so broad as to be institutionalized, so too are today's misbehaviors. Let's consider just a few of them.

First is our government's incessant meddling in other countries. Yes, I understand that in many cases if the United States military weren't in some of those places (133 countries as of the time of this writing!) there would be anarchy and innocent people would suffer. I also understand the theory that our presence around the world is key to our security at home. However, our military is a weapon of destruction, and it is rightfully and thankfully good at it! Therefore, when it is interspersed around the globe at the whim of government officials over which the people of America have little or no control (and many times not even any knowledge), we are placing a match near the powder keg. The United States is not and should not be the police of the world. We cannot afford it financially or politically. Thousands of incidents that go unreported to the American people serve to inflame populations against us. Some of these may arguably be necessary, but the vast majority are not. When an American G.I.'s life is in danger, and he or she has a near impossible task to distinguish friend from foe in a strange land, he or she cannot be blamed for the death of "innocents." The real question is whether or not the G.I. should be put into that position in the first place. If we are going to ask an American youth to be in such a precarious situation, we had better do two things: 1) be absolutely sure their life is worth risking by placing them there 2) defend them when they make the decisions we have trained them to make!

This brings us to the trampling of our ideals in the name of the fight against terrorism. Again, don't get me wrong. I don't believe in using kid's gloves when dealing with thugs. But once we suspend the rights of habeas corpus and start eliminating the rights of United States citizens to trials, representation, and the rule of law, we have become as bad as the terrorists we fight, and have surrendered our principles in the name of protecting them! The ends never justify the means. When the government decides that it can do away with the rights of one group of citizens to protect those of another, how can we ever be sure they won't change the equation of who is protected and who isn't? I personally feel very uncomfortable when our government tells us it is exercising an extra-aggressive privilege for the "greater good."

Next comes the financial meddling by our government. The Federal Reserve lowers interest rates by printing more money. Each time this happens the money you and I have goes down in value. We can buy less with what we have. Meanwhile, the government contractors and financial institutions who receive this newly printed money get rich by receiving the money first and being able to spend it before prices go up. This effectively becomes just another tax on the honest, hard-working American who happens to NOT have access to government cheese. This same average American has to pay enormous taxes to finance not only the worldwide military complex mentioned above but to support the gigantic American entitlement-welfare state. This welfare state has grown up because politicians have gotten good at "selling votes" by promising special interest groups, campaign contributors, and inside dealers government programs that will "fix" their problems. Our federal budget is literally bulging with appropriations for things the government was never intended to do.

Laws, laws, and more laws. Taxes, taxes, and more taxes. And each and every day Americans lose a few more inches of their freedom. The "Republicrats" in Washington collude together to make it all work. Anyone who comes along and calls a spade a spade gets hammered down like a heretic in a religious cult.

Rome was originally a Republic. The structure of its government was able to contain its competing power factions for almost five hundred years. But finally, when the power struggle got too tough and dangerous, the people cried out for a savior. Tyranny to them was better than anarchy. So it became an Empire. Its people had traded freedom for security, and ended up with neither. Then the Empire collapsed, largely under the aggressions of populations it had suppressed, harassed, and mistreated for centuries. At the same time its own people had lost their streak of independence and valor, having lived for centuries under totalitarian rule, till there was no population willing to fight for the preservation of something that had oppressed them in the first place. What began as a passionate Republic ended in tragic indifference. It is nearly impossible not to draw at least a small parallel between the history of Rome and the current United States. Such comparisons are not perfect, of course, but they offer warnings of at least some validity.

If we look to government to solve problems it has created, we are like a hypochondriac taking more and more medicines to counteract the side effects of others we have already taken. Eventually, we become addicted and numb, with barely enough energy to put on our togas and make our way to the Campus Martius to vote for yet another droid promising "change." It is time to stop medicating our symptoms by taking more of what caused our ailments in the first place. We must address the problem at its roots.

Millions of Americans have died on bloody battlefields defending ideals we won't even protect at the voting booth.

232

Freedom is under fire. Undefended, it cannot stand forever. **Millions of Americans have died on bloody battlefields defending ideals we won't even protect at the voting booth.** We have largely progressed from Republic to Empire. Now the "barbarians" around the world are agitated and spoiling for a fight. At the same time, apathy and gullibility are riding high at home. Meanwhile, the government grows in size and power, creeping, ever creeping . . . .

I want neither a Caesar nor a Hun for my master.

I want the Constitution. It was meant to restrain the government, not me.

CYCLE OF DEMOCRACY AND ALEXANDER FRASER TYLER

The following quote is believed to originate with Alexander Fraser Tyler (Tytler in original Scottish). Regardless of who said it, I believe it is worthy of repeating and expounding in relation to present-day America. I do not write this in an attacking spirit, but in a spirit of searching for the right path in a world wandering down blind alleys.

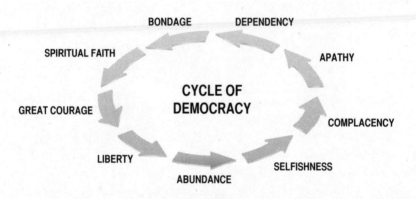

"A democracy cannot exist as a permanent form of government. It can only exist until the voters discover they can vote themselves largesse from the public treasury. From that moment on, the majority always votes for the candidates promising them the most benefits from the public treasury, with the result that a democracy always collapses over a louse fiscal responsibility, always followed by a dictatorship. The average of the world's great civilizations before they decline has been 200 years. These nations have progressed in this sequence:"

Here is Tyler's *Cycle of Democracy* step by step, with my thoughts on America in each step of the cycle.

1. From Bondage to Spiritual Faith;

The Great Awakening of the 1730s in the American colonies was a time of revival and spiritual longing. Jonathon Edwards, considered by many to be America's greatest mind at the time, led the revival with Biblical sermons and a fire for truth. Edwards taught the unvarnished truth about sinful man and our accountability to an Almighty God. Not surprisingly, he is mocked and laughed at today, but that is more of an indictment of our current society than Edward's preaching. Pastor Edwards' magnum opus, *Freedom of the Will,* has never been successfully refuted by any scholar. This work became a critical step in developing the conviction to fear God and not man. Even if "man" in this case happened to be the largest empire in the world upon which the sun never set; the British empire.

2. From Spiritual Faith to Great Courage;

Spiritual faith leads to great courage because one develops convictions for which sacrifice is deemed worthy. A person who does not stand for something will fall for anything. Think of the true heroes throughout history. One of the uniting principles that all heroes have is a willingness to stand for truth and convictions in a world of untruth and apathy. The founding families had great courage to stand for the truth against tyranny and oppression. They did this because they knew the Bible said, "Where the Spirit of the Lord is, there is Liberty." The British were moving in the direction of excessive taxation (2 %) and the colonists would not sit back and allow an off-site government to tax a people without representation.

3. From Courage to Liberty;

The colonial defeat of the British was not a defeat of British military forces as much as a victory over British will. The colonists were fighting for their deeply held principles for which they were willing to risk their life, wealth and sacred honor. The British were fighting for some extra taxation in one of their many colonies. The American will defeated the British will because of an imbalance in the convictions involved. With the defeat of Cornwallis and the subsequent genius of our American Constitution, liberty reigned in the United States under a precious concept called the Rule of Law.

4. From Liberty to Abundance;

The abundance generated by free enterprise and limited government was one of America's biggest blessings, but also one of its biggest challenges. One of the few standing economies after WWII was that of the United States. American products flowed to nearly all foreign markets creating the wealthiest society in the world's history. It takes incredible discipline to remember where blessings come from when abundance is heaped upon further abundance. Over time, people forget the principles that created the liberty because they become too captivated enjoying the fruit of that liberty. Seeing the inequalities in the blessings of individual citizens, an envy of others begins to germinate. People begin wanting equality of results instead of equality of opportunity. The fruit of this unholy thinking is a desire to take the abundance of our brothers and sisters and give it to those "less abounding."

5. From Abundance to Selfishness;

The 1960s were a decade of self masquerading as care for others. Free love, destruction of society's norms, and a drug culture prevailed in the youth. The 1960s were a rebellion against the plastic society of abundance without the belief in the principles that created that abundance. The church, having lost conviction of the truths of the Bible, ossified into an ineffective, retreating "bunker" culture within America. With little truth in the Church, the youth were left on their own to search for answers to the hypocrisy that engulfed them. Instead of returning to the Biblical principles and the God that created the blessings, society entered into the worship of self and self-actualization. The youth of the 1960s saw the hypocrisy, but in their endless faith in their own infallibility marched America even further from its Biblical roots.

6. From Selfishness to Complacency;

Without a Biblical foundation the rebellion in America was bound to produce worse fruits than the plastic culture it attempted to replace. With no firm convictions to stand upon, the rebellion dissolved into the pursuit of peace and personal affluence. The loss of Biblical absolutes is bound to lead from convictions to surrender to complacency as no one is sure what the truth is. What is the use of standing for anything, if we are not sure that what we are standing for is truth? The 1970s saw this complacency as the youth joined the "system" and pursued peace and affluence with little understanding of the original principles upon which America was founded.

7. From Complacency to Apathy;

The 1980s were a brief respite in the cycle. Thanks to the leadership and convictions of Ronald Reagan, America stood its ground against Communism and proved that Communism was a paper tiger. The respite was short lived because the President, even with his bully pulpit, cannot consistently educate Americans on Biblical truths. This must be a function of the church, which has abdicated its responsibility in an effort to be more relative to a lost generation.

The 1990s saw a near complete surrender to apathy and personal fulfillment. With a rejection of absolute values people defined their own values and pursued fulfillment in the myriad of choices available to them. People did not care who was running the government as long as they were left alone to pursue the own personal agenda. The government began forming focus groups to ascertain what the people wanted and focused more than ever on giving it to them, surrendering all leadership responsibilities to the disparate wishes of the people and their special interests. Government, instead of playing the role of umpire and defender of our freedoms, began to play the role of a benevolent dictator. The dictator studied to learn what we wanted and offered that to us with only a presumed token price of submission to the almighty sovereignty of government in the affairs of the citizens.

8. From Apathy to Dependency;

The 2000s will be remembered as the decade of complete submission to the government's largesse. The American citizens depend upon government for their welfare, health care, and social security. It would be unthinkable for most Americans to live without the direct involvement of our beneficent Big Brother. The price of dependency is submission of our freedoms to the dictates of Big Brother. The old saying that you boil a frog one degree at a time aptly fits here. If you take a frog and throw him into boiling water, the frog will have enough sense to jump out. But if you turn up the temperature slowly, the frog will open up its pores and will literally be boiled without an attempted escape. Americans are now boiling in our dependency on government.

9. From Dependency back again to Bondage.

Eventually in our dependence, we see our status falling in the free world as slaves can never perform the functions of free men and women. Although the government still mouths the words of our founding fathers, the words have new meanings. The citizens cannot put a finger on the malady, but they know something is not right. In their desperation, they look for a messiah to save them. Because the churches are not sharing the message of the true messiah and the true way to liberty, the citizens look for a worldly messiah. A perceptive leader, with words that tickle the ears promises to be the searched for messiah. With our republican form of government torn asunder and transformed into a nascent democracy – the powerful words and promises of deliverance speak directly to the masses. A savior is born unto the people and salvation is promised in the form of more and ever-encroaching government programs.

A shocking truth is learned too late: Man cannot save man and only Jesus Christ can liberate the soul in bondage. A people held in bondage to sin can never be responsible to run a free government. The people in bondage will look to the government the way Christians look to their Savior. Government cannot be the savior to the people and was never intended to be so when created by our founders. America's national debt is now over $15 trillion and to service the interest on the debt is over $450 billion per year. This makes interest on debt the third biggest item on our government's budget. We are bankrupting our children's inheritance on the altar of self indulgence.

I did not write this to scare people into inactivity, but to awaken our consciences to the choices that face us. We do not have to complete this cycle, and just as Ronald Reagan interrupted the cycle, we can too. Will it take convictions and guts? Yes, but a Godly people that have studied the truth of our founding principles will not be swayed by the promises of an almighty government. Examine yourself on these issues. Where do you stand at this historic time?

Let me close with one of my brother's favorite authors. The science fiction writer, Robert Heinlein called this issue we've been discussing "Bread and Circuses" - a reference to the Roman Emperors providing food and entertainment to distract the masses from the tyranny they were under. In *To Sail beyond the Sunset* the character Lazarus Long discusses this problem:

"A perfect democracy, a 'warm body' democracy in which every adult may vote and all votes count equally has no internal feedback for self correction. It depends solely on the wisdom and self-restraint of citizens . . . which is opposed by the folly and lack of self-restraint of other citizens. What is supposed to happen in a democracy is that each sovereign citizen will always vote in the public interest for the safety and welfare of all. But what does happen is that he votes his own self-interest as he sees it . . . which for the majority translates as 'Bread and Circuses.'

Bread and Circuses is the cancer of democracy, the fatal disease for which there is no cure. Democracy often works beautifully at first. But once a state extends the franchise to every warm body, be he producer or parasite, that day marks the beginning of the end of the state. For when the plebs discover that they can vote themselves bread and circuses without limit and that the productive members of the body politic cannot stop them, they will do so, until the state bleeds to death or in its weakened condition the state succumbs to an invader--the barbarians enter Rome."

The Biblical passage from Hosea 4:6-10 captures the crossroads where America stands at this moment:

"My people are destroyed for lack of knowledge.
Because you have rejected knowledge,
I also will reject you from being priest for Me;
Because you have forgotten the law of your God,
I also will forget your children.
The more they increased,
The more they sinned against Me;
I will change their glory into shame.
They eat up the sin of My people;
They set their heart on their iniquity.
And it shall be: like people, like priest.
So I will punish them for their ways,
And reward them for their deeds.
For they shall eat, but not have enough;
They shall commit harlotry, but not increase;
Because they have ceased obeying the LORD."

Let freedom never perish in your hands. - *Joseph Addison*

I believe there are more instances of the abridgment of the freedom of the people by gradual and silent encroachments of those in power than by violent and sudden usurpations. - James Madison

Freedom has a thousand charms to show, that slaves, howe'er contented, never know. - William Cowper

The contest for ages has been to rescue liberty from the grasp of executive power. - Daniel Webster

Men fight for liberty and win it with hard knocks. Their children, brought up easy, let it slip away again, poor fools. And their grandchildren are once more slaves. - D.H. Lawrence

SUGGESTED READING LIST

The following titles comprise an abbreviated reading list recommended for deeper insight into the main categories of this book. It is by no means an exhaustive compilation but consists of the works which had the biggest impact upon the authors' education to this point. For further recommendations and reviews please visit the authors' Internet blogs: www.chrisbrady.com, orrin1woodward.wordpress.com

Attitude and Success
See You at the Top, Zig Zigglar
The Greatest Salesman in the World, Og Mandino
Wooden: A Lifetime of Observations On and Off the Court, John Wooden
The Psychology of Winning, Dennis Waitley
Life is Tremendous, Charlie "Tremendous" Jones

People Skills and Principles
How to Have Power and Confidence in Dealing With People, Les Giblin
How to Win Friends and Influence People, Dale Carnegie
Personality Plus, Florence Littauer
Bringing Out the Best in People, Alan Lloyd McGinnis
The 7 Habits of Highly Effective People, Stephen Covey

Leadership
It's Your Ship, Captain D. Michael Abrashoff
The Cycle of Leadership, Noel Tichy

The World's Most Powerful Leadership Principle,
    James C. Hunter
The 21 Irrefutable Laws of Leadership, John C. Maxwell
Launching a Leadership Revolution, Chris Brady and Orrin
    Woodward (it's a summary of so much of our learning!)

Historical Leadership Illustrations
The Founding Fathers on Leadership, Don T. Phillips
Scuttle Your Ships Before Advancing, Richard Luecke
Churchill on Leadership, Steven Hayward
Character Counts, Os Guiness
The American Leadership Tradition, Marvin Olasky

The History of Liberty
The Future of Freedom, Fareed Zakaria
The 5000 Year Leap: The Miracle That Changed the World,
    W. Cleon Skousen
How the West was Lost, Alexander Boot
The Conservative Mind, Russell Kirk
The Passion of the Western Mind, Richard Tarnas

Economics
The Economy in Mind, Warren T. Brookes
Economics in One Lesson, Henry Hazlitt
The Making of Modern Economics, Mark Skousen
Human Action, Ludwig von Mises
The New Empire of Debt, Bonner/Wigan

Politics and Governance
Politics: Easy as P.I.E., Bob McEwen
The Revolt of the Masses, Jose Ortega y Gasset
The Road to Serfdom, F. A. Hayek
The Creature from Jekyll Island, G. Edward Griffin
Slouching Towards Gomorrah, Robert H. Bork

SUBSCRIPTIONS

LIFE SERIES

Our lives are lived out in the eight categories of Faith, Family, Finances, Fitness, Following, Freedom, Friends, and Fun. The monthly LIFE Series of 4 audios and 1 book is specifically designed to bring you life-transforming information in each of these areas. Whether you are interested in one or two of these, or all eight, you will be delighted with timeless truths and effective strategies for living a life of excellence, brought to you in an entertaining, intelligent, well-informed, and insightful manner. It has been said that it may be your life, but it's not yours to waste. Subscribe to the LIFE Series today and learn how to make yours count!

The LIFE Series – dedicated to helping people grow in each of the 8 F categories: Faith, Family, Finances, Fitness, Following, Freedom, Friends, and Fun.
4 audios and 1 book are shipped each month.
$50.00 plus S&H
Pricing is valid for both USD and CAD.

LLR SERIES

Everyone will be called upon to lead at some point in life—and often at many points. The question is whether people will be ready when they are called. The LLR Series is based on the *New York Times* bestseller *Launching a Leadership Revolution*, in which authors Chris Brady and Orrin Woodward teach about leadership in a way that applies to everyone. Whether you are seeking corporate or business advancement, community influence, church impact, or better stewardship and effectiveness in your home, the principles and specifics taught in the LLR Series will equip you with what you need.

Subscribers receive 4 audios and 1 leadership book each month. Topics covered include finances, leadership, public speaking, attitude, goal setting, mentoring, game planning, accountability and progress tracking, levels of motivation, levels of influence, and leaving a personal legacy.

Subscribe to the LLR Series and begin applying these life-transforming truths today!

The LLR (Launching a Leadership Revolution) Series – dedicated to helping people grow in their leadership ability.
4 audios and 1 book are shipped each month.
$50.00 plus S&H
Pricing is valid for both USD and CAD.

Don't Miss Out on the 3 for FREE Program!

When a Customer or Member subscribes to any one or more packages, that person is given the incentive to attract other subscribers as well. Once a subscriber signs up three or more Customers on equivalent or greater dollar value subscriptions, that person will receive his or her next month's subscription FREE!

AGO SERIES

Whether you have walked with Christ your entire life or have just begun the journey, we welcome you to experience the love, joy, understanding, and purpose that only Christ can offer. This series is designed to touch and nourish the hearts of all faith levels. Gain valuable support and guidance from our top speakers and special guests that will help you enhance your understanding of God's plan for your life, marriage, children, and character. Nurture your soul, strengthen your faith, and find answers on the go or quietly at home with the AGO Series.

The AGO (All Grace Outreach) Series – dedicated to helping people grow spiritually. 1 audio and 1 book are shipped each month. $25.00 plus S&H Pricing is valid for both USD and CAD.

EDGE SERIES

Designed especially for those on the younger side of life, this is a hard-core, no-frills approach to learning the things that make for a successful life.

Eliminate the noise around you about who you are and who you should become. Instead, figure it out for yourself in a mighty way with life-changing information from people who would do just about anything to have learned these truths much, much sooner in life. Get access on a monthly basis to wisdom and knowledge that it took them a lifetime to discover!

Edge Series – dedicated to helping young people grow in their leadership ability. 1 audio is shipped each month. $10.00 plus S&H Pricing is valid for both USD and CAD.

FREEDOM SERIES

Attention all freedom lovers: Gain an even greater understanding of the significance and power of freedom, stay informed about the issues that affect your own freedom, and find out what you can do to reverse any decline and lead the world toward greater liberty with the LIFE Leadership Freedom Series!

Freedom Series – dedicated to helping people understand the meaning and value of freedom. 1 audio is shipped each month. $10.00 plus S&H
Pricing is valid for both USD and CAD.

LIFE LIBRARY

The LIFE Library is your round-the-clock resource for LIFE Leadership's latest and greatest leadership content in either video or audio format. And you never have to be quiet in this library!

WATCH, LISTEN, LEARN, AND GROW!

- Audio and video content covering LIFE Leadership's 8 Fs (Faith, Family, Finances, Fitness, Following, Freedom, Friends, and Fun)
- New exclusive content added every month
- Material from industry leaders, including bestselling authors Orrin Woodward and Chris Brady and LIFE Coaches Tim Marks and Claude Hamilton
- Option to read reviews and share your own insights
- Ability to create a list of favorites for quick and easy retrieval
- A feature that allows you to search by format, speaker, and/or subject

$40.00 per month
Pricing is valid for both USD and CAD.

RASCAL RADIO

Listen up! You asked for it, and we heard you loud and clear.
Now hear this: Rascal Radio is a one-of-a-kind, personal-
development Internet radio hot spot. Switch on and tune
in to an incredible selection of preset stations for each of
LIFE Leadership's 8 Fs that you can customize by choosing
a combination of speaker or subject. The life-changing
possibilities are endless as you browse through the hundreds
of audio recordings available. Select and purchase your
favorite talks to gift to family and friends. Listen, learn, and
grow through the ease of Rascal Radio.

Subscription includes a 7-Day FREE Trial.
$49.95 per month

FREE Rascal Radio Smartphone App Available!

LIFE LIVE

The dynamic, world-class LIFE Live
educational events are designed to inform,
equip, and train you for success in a
powerful way.

Ranging in size from a couple hundred to
thousands of participants all across North
America, these fun, energy-packed events
deliver life-changing information from LIFE
Leadership's 8 F categories (Faith, Family,
Finances, Fitness, Following, Freedom,
Friends, and Fun).

$40.00 per month
Pricing is valid for both USD and CAD.